INTERNET

shopping

Andrew Adamides

kandour Ltd

Published by
Kandour Ltd
1-3 Colebrooke Place
London N1 8HZ
United Kingdom

This edition printed in 2005 for
Bookmart Ltd
Registered Number 2372865
Trading As Bookmart Ltd
Blaby Road
Wigston
Leicester LE18 4SE

First published March 2005

Created for Kandour Ltd by Metro Media Ltd
Author: Andrew Adamides
Cover and text design: Paul Barton
Page layout: Chris Readlamb and Lee Coventry
Managing editor: Jenny Ross
Photography: photos.com

Printed and bound in United Kingdom

ISBN 1-904756-38-7

INTRODUCTION

Love it or hate it, the internet is many things – a home to information, from the life-altering to the trivial; a channel for communication and a source of addiction, annoyance and amazement. It's also one of the hottest – and undoubtedly the biggest – shopping centres in the world.

Since the web started becoming a part of everyday life, the number of sites using it to sell has mushroomed. There are now countless shopping sites, from huge corporations down to one-horse amateurs, and forecasts tell us the number of sellers going online is only going to increase.

Projections estimate that by the end of this year, almost 10 per cent of UK retail sales will happen over the internet – at a value of almost £20 billion.

But with so many shops – and other selling formats – available to choose from, where do you even start? Should you buy at auction, from a discount shop or a famous high street name that's now online as well? How do you compare prices and make sure you're not getting ripped off? Is buying online safe? What about selling. Should you put your items on eBay or get yourself a server and set up your own site? And what exactly is a server?

Starting at the very beginning with simple step-by-step explanations of how the buying process works, this book outlines the different types of online retailer, tells you how to find them, how to make sure they're trustworthy, and how to check that when you do buy, you're buying at the best price possible.

It explains auctions and bidding, and covers different sectors of the retail market, giving you all the goods on buying clothes, antiques, cars and even property online. There are also sections on the different ways to pay for items bought online, and how to 'pay safe'.

The book also takes a look at selling, giving you an overview of how to run an online auction, and the basics on what you'll need to do if you want to start selling through a dedicated website of your own.

Finally, it also tells you what to do if things do go wrong, and how to complain most effectively if you find yourself falling victim to a site that doesn't deliver.

There's no doubt that internet shopping is here to stay – and with this book, you'll be able to make informed decisions about how and where to buy online.

THE PROS & CONS OF SHOPPING ONLINE

Well, who would have thought it? That a communications system designed for the military to withstand a nuclear war back in the late 1960s, would end up being the world's biggest shopping window. Since the internet, or more importantly the world wide web began, the number of people using it to shop has skyrocketed at an astonishing rate, proving that online sellers must be doing something right. In fact, it could be argued that such are the benefits of online shopping that you could actually consider abandoning your local high street altogether.

For a start, the one thing us consumers loathe is the ancient practice of queuing. With the net, you won't be forced to stand in a line for eons with your purchase behind someone for whom personal hygiene is a mere concept rather than a reality. It's just a case of clicking on a button and waiting for the item to arrive at your door (or download onto your computer, depending on what you're buying).

Secondly, there's the convenience factor. Whatever you're looking to purchase, you can do it from the comfort of your own home – just log on and start searching the net straight away, bypassing the torrential rain or that jostle for a parking space. Of course, the net's 24-hour nature also means that you can shop at any time of the day or night. While shopping in the real world demands that you conform to its time frame, internet shopping conforms to yours. Don't get off work until after the shops close? No problem – if you're buying online, you can do it at three in the morning. If you really must.

It's also far more convenient for tracking down those hard-to-find buys; a fruitless online search for that elusive item involves far less effort than trekking round your local shops. And with the huge variety of stores plying their wares online, you're bound to come across whatever it is you're looking for anyway. Prices are often lower on the internet too, as online retailers have fewer overheads to pay. Oh, and there aren't any annoying shop assistants to hassle you either (or blind you with their sometimes staggering ignorance of their store's product range).

There are, however, a few drawbacks. Firstly, you do need to be careful with some consumer items where appearance is a factor.

While almost all online retailers show pictures of the items they're selling, furniture or clothing colours can differ from that perfect picture on your monitor and real life. Similarly, sizing can be an issue with clothes, which you won't be able to try on before you buy.

Also, there's shipping costs to consider. Since items will have to be sent to you, these need to be figured into your final costing – especially for large items. Yes, prices will often be lower if you buy online, but the cost of delivery can sometimes negate that saving completely. Unlike regular shopping, internet shopping also doesn't offer instant access to your purchase either (unless it's instantly downloadable). So, you'll have to wait for the item to be delivered, which can take a few days or longer.

Customer services may also not be instant either. While a few sellers do have live interactive help available – either in the form of human helpers on instant messenger or sophisticated computers programmed to answer most questions – most online retailers don't. Hence if you do want help, you'll be limited to either the Frequently Asked Questions section or e-mailing the customer services centre. While many online shops do offer a phone-based helpline, be warned that these calls can be costly.

Finally, while the threat of internet credit card theft running rampant has proved to be less of a problem than initially stated by scare-mongering tabloids, there is always the danger of hackers stealing sensitive personal and financial information. Such risks can be minimised by savvy shopping though, and thefts like these are probably no less likely to occur than they would in the real world.

But let's face it – if you're smart, the pros of online shopping can far outweigh the cons. So what are you waiting for? You have a computer, an internet connection, a credit/debit card and a basic knowledge of how to use the internet. But where do you start your online shopping spree?

 Finding online outlets and their different types

Finding online sellers is generally very easy. The best known, like Amazon, advertise in numerous publications and on television, and you can access their websites simply by typing in their URL (usually the seller's name) plus either .com or .co.uk, depending on where you are located. Many will also redirect users who type in the URL slightly incorrectly. Alternately, you can use Google or another powerful search engine to search for the seller's name.

This will usually bring up their homepage as the first entry in the search results page.

But what if you don't know where to go and buy something or you're looking for a shop selling a particular type of item? In such cases, you'll want to go for the first of our online seller types – the online mall.

Online malls

While the internet boasts numerous 'star' brands, there are also countless other sellers, all much smaller, who can offer a potential bargain on whatever it is you're looking for. Often, these are the retailers who sell less exciting products, like electrical appliances, rather than entertainment or fashion-related items.

In order to help consumers find these smaller sites, online malls have sprung up on the net. These function in much the same way as real shopping malls do where you find many shops grouped together in one convenient location – but with an online mall, you'll find them in the form of links to the shops' own websites.

Links will usually be arranged by category, which is another plus over real-life malls. It means shops selling similar items will all be grouped together, whereas in a physical shopping centre, they'll likely be as far apart as they can get from their competitors. Whether you've found that shop through an online mall or have gone directly to a retailer's homepage, you'll find that most of the sellers will be one of three different types:

Online-only shops

These are retailers who do not have any sort of presence in the 'real world'. For example, you won't find Amazon on your local high street. Such retailers sell exclusively through their websites and deliver products to you by mail. All customer service is done electronically or via the telephone. The benefit of such set-ups is that they don't need to spend money on creating an actual real world shop, so their prices are often lower.

The potential downside though is that, if the retailer isn't reputable, chasing them up in the unlikely event that something goes wrong can prove to be more difficult, as their head offices can be much harder to locate. All online selling websites should have clear details about their customer service provisions, and if they don't, then simply avoid buying from them. Also, look to see if the online retailer has its head office address listed too – you'll usually find it in their 'About Us' section.

Online-outlets of 'real world' shops

The growing popularity of internet shopping has seen high street retailers jumping on the online bandwagon and setting up their own websites to complement their physical stores. Like online-only shops, these sites feature web-based catalogues of their merchandise; the difference being that they'll have the same items in their actual shops, so you can go along and see your potential purchase in the flesh before buying.

Many of these will also offer online-only deals with prices that can't be found in their retail shops. Often these bargains will be on end-of-line or reconditioned items and can offer good value for money. Some will also offer the option of choosing home delivery or having the items sent to a conveniently nearby branch for collection.

Do be aware though that while most retailers do sell through their websites, some do not and just offer online catalogues of their items plus information about branch locations, opening times and charges, etc. The websites of 'real' shops will usually provide this sort of information anyway whether they sell through the net or not, and it can be extremely useful even if all you want is to locate your nearest branch – as well as find out whether an item is in stock or not. Many people do, in fact, use the internet to do their research on a product before going out and buying it in the real world.

Manufacturer websites

Many makers now sell their products directly to the public through their own websites. This is because previously, most did not have their own shops because of the sheer expense, and opted instead to flog their goods through resellers. While a few manufacturers such as Nike or Nokia do buck this trend by having their own physical stores, their brand-specific shops tend to be only located in major cities to ensure that enough customers pass through their doors; this makes them pretty much off-limits if you don't live in a shopper-friendly metropolis. Adding an online shop to a manufacturer's website, however, is far easier and cheaper, and many makers have done just this. Finding a manufacturer's website is easy; most use their name, followed by the .com, .co.uk or whatever suffix is specific to your particular country. For companies with numerous brands grouped together under one umbrella, you may find yourself forwarded to a website with their most famous name on it. Electrolux, for example, comes under the Zanussi brand in the UK.

Buying direct from the manufacturer also has its pros and cons. You may well get slightly cheaper prices as the makers will not have the overheads of most resellers. However, the items sold may be limited, and delivery options will generally be fairly pricy. There may, however, be bargains on obsolete or reconditioned equipment, and these should still come with a full warranty.

Not all manufacturers sell through their websites, however. Those that do, tend to sell smaller, more easily-delivered items – a general rule of thumb is that if the item can be posted or couriered, then you

will probably be able to buy from the manufacturer, but if it needs to be delivered by deliverymen, then you won't.

Manufacturer websites can, however, be an excellent place to research product ranges. This is especially true with very large consumer items like cars, where websites now have all but replaced paper brochures, as advances in technology mean you can usually view models in all colours, study specification lists and often customise to your heart's content. Typically, you can then be given a price right there and then for the vehicle you have specified.

Many manufacturers can also help you get a finance quote online, check stock lists and refer you to your nearest dealer. Even those manufacturer websites that don't sell their own products directly may sell smaller accessories for them. Do be aware though that product ranges can differ from country to country – so be sure to shop on the manufacturer's website that's specific to your own country.

Makers with their headquarters based abroad, may well have a main website which lists all the items they produce, and others which are country-specific. Nothing, though, is more annoying than setting your heart on a certain mobile phone that's depicted in all its 3D glory on the maker's website - only to find it is not available outside the US, for example. But once you've found the shop you're looking for how should you proceed?

Buying – step-by-step

Most online shops allow you to start shopping directly from their front page. With manufacturer websites, you will have to look for the link to their 'Online Shop', 'Web Shop' or similar. If you can't find this, click on the link marked 'Site Map' as this will show you a list of all the places you can go to on the site, and should display the shop (if there is one) prominently.

Depending on what sort of retailer they are, most online sellers will begin by offering direct links from their front page to their various product sectors. For example, the online retailer of electrical goods will have links to their sections on computers, TVs, DVD Players, etc. They will also have any 'specials' advertised on their front page with direct links to the particular promotion.

Once you click on the relevant category, you'll find items organised in different ways depending on the size of the retailer and how many of a particular item they're selling. For example, if the seller has only five different models of microwave oven on their site, then you will probably find a list of these, all clickable.

On this page, there may be 'tick boxes' and a 'Compare' button. Ticking these boxes and clicking 'Compare' should give you a side-by-side view of the selected items, their specifications and prices so that you can compare them and see which offers the best value for your needs. If, though, the site carries five different brands of microwaves, each with five different models available, you will probably find a further subcategory featuring the manufacturer names before you can actually access specific models. You may also come across an option to show items by price; this allows you to examine comparable models from different ranges side-by-side.

Most sellers' sites usually feature search engines that allow you to browse for information, and these will function in a similar way to Google, Yahoo or any other search engine. Sellers' search engines do vary in sophistication; the most basic will allow you to put in keywords such as 'microwave oven', and will bring up a list of all the microwave ovens for sale on the site with links to their respective pages.

Others, however, allow you to be more specific; a sophisticated search engine will allow you to key in the features you want. For example, you can search specifically for Zanussi and Candy electric (not gas) hobs in the £150-£300 range that come in white and have four hotplates. The obvious benefit of such search engines is that they allow you to save time if you already know the details about a particular product, or if you know the exact make and model – you can simply enter such information and go directly to the item's page on the site.

Search engines are far more important when the site specialises in one particular area and has a myriad of products available. For example, a site like Amazon carries thousands of book titles in many categories, and browsing the 'Adventure Novel' section alone would take hours. Hence, good search engines will allow customers to search by keywords, or for a particular writer. In the latter's case, the results of this search will often include a side panel with suggestions pointing to other authors that the customer may enjoy.

Once you've searched the site for suitable items and found something you think you might like to buy, you'll want to take a good look at it. One of the big drawbacks of the online shopping experience though is that unless you go out and look at an identical item for sale in a shop, you may not get a clear idea of what it is you are paying out for. This kind of risk usually applies to items like clothing or furniture.

After all, the colours of the shirt that caught your eye may look decidedly different in reality when compared to what you saw up on your monitor screen. Also, as we all know, size does matter – for instance, fashion label A may state 'small', and its shirt will fit you perfectly, but fashion label B, offering the same 'small' option, may require the Atkins Diet in order for you to fit into it properly. Having said that, you do run a similar risk when dealing with mail-order catalogues, or when buying from a catalogue shop.

Items such as electrical goods, branded toys and DVDs, though, are no-brainers – their effectiveness really isn't based on variable factors like colour or style and, unless you are sent the wrong item, what you see on screen will be what you get – unless you didn't check out that specs list properly before ordering.

Browsing product information on a shopping website is one area where internet shopping really does have a bona fide advantage over real world stores. Specifications for a product are usually set out in an easy-to-read (and printable) list, and such a breakdown is especially useful with electrical goods such as personal computers.

Indeed, as the internet has become more sophisticated, so too has the amount of visual information you can get on a product. Where once a page on a product might have had just one small picture of it, most sites now offer pop-up super-sized images, showing much larger high-resolution pictures.

With so many expensive consumer items selling on their appearance, many products also have animated images which show, for example, how a mobile phone cover slides or flips open. You'll also be able to change the look of the phone, so you can see what it looks like in all the different finishes available. On vehicle manufacturer websites, it is now common to have images of cars where the colours can not only be changed at the click of a button, but which you can 'click and drag' to make the vehicle rotate 360 degrees in order to see it from all angles. Auto makers also regularly offer downloadable films of their vehicles in action – indeed, some car makers like BMW have commissioned high-flying Hollywood directors in the past to produce short online-only films featuring their products.

Of course, not all sites will feature such technology or special promotions, and how 'intricately' you get to look at an item usually depends on how expensive and desirable the product is – as well as on the retailer itself; the bigger the company, the better their web presentation usually is. If you're buying a bargain basement electrical item, don't go expecting all-singing, all-dancing 3D views of a cut-price toaster! The most you'll get is a super-size image, or a row of pictures showing the different colours the item's available in. Once you have been seduced by either the price of the product (or by its dazzling online presentation), you can purchase it by clicking on the link for 'Buy' or 'Buy Now'. In most cases, the item you've selected will then be placed into your 'shopping cart' or 'basket'. This shopping cart acts much like a supermarket trolley or basket – you place items in it and 'carry' it around with you while selecting more items, before heading for the checkout. The website then 'remembers' what you ordered while you were browsing the other pages on the site.

After heading for the checkout, sophisticated sites will often ask you to create a password-protected account. This account will securely store your delivery address, details of the credit card you're using for the transaction, and other relevant information. This might sound intrusive but it'll save you time if you decide to shop at the same place in the future – after all, they'll now have your info on file so you can order

without the hassle of typing in all those pesky details again. It also means that they can offer you 'personalised' advertising of products they think will be of interest to you based on your past purchases. Whether this is a blessing or a curse is open to debate.

Once you have signed up like this, you can place items in your cart indefinitely in some cases – you can leave the site, return days later and find that they are still in your basket. If you're not signed in though and surf away from the site to return much later, you may well find your basket empty again, and if you switch off your computer, it will most definitely be empty. This is because in order to save your items, the site uses 'cookies'. These are temporary computer programs that are downloaded to your hard-drive to keep track of your order, and they can last for varying periods of time depending on your and the seller's computer settings. Simply logging off the net or switching off your computer could mean the cookies being erased – thus requiring you to start all over again.

However, assuming that you intend to purchase two items during the same visit, item A will remain in your cart while you seek out item B. You can, of course, change your mind at any time, and removing an item from your cart is as simple as putting it in – in the panel giving details of what's in your cart, there should be details of each item with a link next to them reading 'Remove From Cart' or similar.

If there are two or more items in your cart, then clicking the 'Remove' button next to one of the items will remove only that particular item. Some sites also have an 'Empty Cart' or 'Remove All Items From Cart' button that throws everything out and allows you to start from scratch. The shopping cart panel also shows the individual cost of each item in your cart and your current total (excluding shipping). Some websites though may limit the amount of items you can add to your cart before proceeding through to the checkout. Most, however, will not, as it's obviously in their interest for you to buy as much as possible from them.

Assuming you don't surf away from the site for too long or switch your computer off, the items will still be in your cart when you decide you want to buy them. To do this, you will need to click on 'Proceed To Checkout' or similar – this button is usually located at the bottom of the shopping cart panel.

If you have never shopped at the site before, the website may ask you to 'create an account' at this point (some rather cheekily ask you to do this when you try to place the first item into your shopping cart so that they can get your details – even if you eventually decide not to buy). You are then usually required to enter your name, address, contact details and details of the credit card you will be using plus its billing address if this is different from the delivery address.

If you have shopped at the site before and are already signed in, then instead of asking for payment and delivery information to be entered, the site will show the information used on your previous visits and ask you to confirm that it is still correct; clicking the

'Confirm' button at the bottom of the page usually does this. There will also be an option to change any pertinent information including your delivery and billing addresses, and credit card details.

Some simpler sites don't operate account systems and won't retain your details – these will simply ask for payment details every time you use them. Generally speaking, the smaller, more independent online retailers will operate like this while larger conglomerates will look to boost business by operating more personalised sites with account features. However the site operates, whenever you put in sensitive information like your credit card number, you should always ensure that the connection is secure in order to avoid any danger of having your information stolen.

During the purchasing process, you will also be asked to select your preferred shipping method. Usually, sellers offering small items that can be sent through the post will have several options available at different costs, and some may offer their slowest option for free. Shops selling large items that require delivery will usually ask you to select a time/date for the delivery to take place from a calendar of available time slots. Again, there may be a charge for this, or it may be free, but the site should make clear what any charge will be. To finalise your purchase, there will be a 'Buy' or 'Buy Now' button. Clicking this will authorise the charge to your credit card and, depending on the speed of your connection and how long it takes the system to contact the card issuer, your purchase should go through within a minute. Often, a 'processing payment, please wait' message will appear, warning you not to close the browser or hit the stop or reload button. Doing so may result in your card being charged without the order being actually placed – or in your card being charged twice.

If something untoward does happen, like your computer freezing or one of the above buttons being hit accidentally, and you subsequently receive no confirmation of the transaction having gone through, then you should contact your card issuer and/or the retailer's customer services department. They will be able to clarify whether or not your order has been placed, and if your card has been charged.

If there is a problem with any of the information you have entered during the purchasing process, then the system will not process the transaction and will take you through to a screen where you can correct your details. It should explain to you what is wrong i.e. if the address you gave does not match the billing address on file for the card, or if the card cannot be verified, etc. This will be the case at any step of the buying process when you make an error or omission; their system will not allow you to proceed without filling in all the information it requires, be it a phone number, e-mail address or delivery option.

If, as in most cases, the transaction goes according to plan, then you will be taken through to a screen that will inform you that your purchase is complete. This will usually give you a breakdown of the purchases made, the cost, and a transaction ID code. It may tell you to print out the page for your records, or to note down the transaction ID code – so it's best to regard this page as your receipt. Most sites will, however, send a duplicate of this receipt to the e-mail address you provided, but it's always wise to either print or save the page just in case this e-mail doesn't arrive for any reason – or is swept up by an overzealous spam filter.

Depending on the item, the receipt will include details of the time frame chosen for shipping, or the delivery date given for larger items. At this point, all you should have to do is wait for your order to arrive. Should there be a problem however, either with the non-arrival of items or with the wrong order being sent, always make sure your receipt – or at least the website – carries prominent details on how to contact the seller's customer services depart-ment. Usually, this will be done either by phone or by e-mail, and they should be able to sort out any problems that occur.

Auctions

Online auctions can thank a most unusual source for their existence – the Pez dispenser. For the uninitiated, Pez dispensers are small plastic dispensers with cartoon character heads on them, which flip open and, in the process eject, one Pez – which is a small piece of shaped candy.

Pez dispensers are widely collected, with some being highly sought-after. In 1995, one Pierre Omidyar, whose wife collected Pez dispensers, saw how she interacted through the internet with other collectors, and had an idea – what if Pez dispensers could be advertised on the internet for a fixed period of time during which people could bid for them, auction-style; the highest bidder at the end of that period being the winner.

From these humble beginnings came eBay, the trading venue for millions of people worldwide. At any one time, there are 19 million items listed on eBay in 35,000 different categories, from VCRs and cars to antique clothing and concert tickets.

Of course, eBay has spawned numerous imitators since it arrived on the scene but many have fallen by the wayside, and none have managed to equal its success. Various sites have tried the auction format and others have tried variations on it; one, for example, had a system whereby items were listed at a certain price, which dropped incrementally every hour. Bidders then had the choice of either buying at the initial high price or sweating it out while they waited for the price to drop further – hoping against hope that nobody else would beat them to it.

Still others launched auction sites specialising in certain types of item; automotive or 'adult' items in particular. However, most of those still operating follow the eBay format and as such are fairly straightforward to use.

You don't need to be registered with eBay to search for items or browse listings, but you do need to be registered if you want to bid. The actual registration process is fairly simple – you fill out a basic form, giving your name, address and contact details, and then create a username and password free of charge. eBay and most other auction sites don't charge buyers for registering because their revenue comes from advertising and from charging sellers a fee to list their items. They also take a percentage of the final bid price. If you wish to sell, you will also have to register a credit card so that eBay can be certain of getting their seller fees.

There are numerous eBay sites for different countries worldwide but all are well integrated. The first was, of course, eBay.com, domiciled in the US, but there are now many others including eBay.co.uk, eBay.it and eBay.fr, and you can access the homepage of each from anywhere in the world. You can also look at the original eBaymotors.com, the specialist car site, from anywhere – although most vehicles on the site are located in the US with the international eBay sites carrying listings for vehicles within their regular categories. Only the eBay Mature Audiences listings featuring adult material cannot be accessed from outside the US, and even within the US, they require bidders to have a credit card on file for proof of age before they can be granted access.

Auction items are listed in categories and sub-categories, but due to the vast number of things on sale at any one time, most people prefer to use eBay's search engine. The engine itself works just like any other; you put in a word (or words) relating to what you are looking for – for example 'Shrek' and 'DVD' – and this will bring up a list of all the copies of Shrek on DVD that have been listed for sale.

A drop-down menu can then be used to sort these by time remaining on the auction, highest price, lowest price, items listed most recently, distance from the bidder, and whether or not the seller accepts PayPal, the online payment system.

The list gives the title or heading of each auction, the current price that the item has been bid up to, the number of bids made, and the time remaining. It will also show which categories the item has been found in, and will give you the option to search within a particular category or its sub-category.

When using the auction site based in your home country, you will have the option to set the search so it looks in either domestic or international settings. When sellers list their items on eBay, they have the option to sell worldwide or to limit the places to where they will send items. Most choose to sell worldwide but some do prefer only to sell to their home country.

Whatever site the seller lists on, if they choose to sell worldwide, their item will appear in the results for searches made on any eBay site. You will also have the option to search the title and the body text of the auction, which will always return more items. The 'Advanced Search' page gives further options including searching by seller's name, bidder's name or by searching completed auctions.

Clicking on the title of an auction will take you through to that item's page. Remember, every item on eBay gets its own page, which is arranged as

follows: At the very top, the category in which the item has been placed is listed. Under this is the item heading or title, which is written by the seller. It's this heading that eBay's standard search will look at to see whether or not an item matches your keywords. Therefore, it's in the seller's best interest to write as much as he or she can, but there is a character limit on headings.

Sellers should include information like the item's name, who made it, when it was made, what model number it is, and so forth – in other words, the most salient information about the item. To the right of the heading will be the item number – this is the number allotted to the item by eBay.

Beneath the heading will be information about the current price the item has been bid up to, the starting price, the number of bids, the identity of the current highest bidder, and how much time is left on the auction. It will also state the item's location, the postage cost to the winning bidder (if this information has been provided), and where the seller is willing to post the item. To the left of this information will be a small picture of the product if the seller has uploaded one (which they should have done, as most items sell very poorly without a picture for prospective bidders to examine). Clicking on this will take you down to the bottom of the page, where a larger version of the photo will appear. There may also be additional pictures of the item if the seller has chosen to include any.

Above the pictures will be a written description of the item, which should include as much detail as possible about the item including its age and condition. A good seller will also include as many further keywords relating to the item as possible, since it is this text which is searched in addition to the title when the 'Search Title And Description' box is ticked.

Beneath this description will be full postage and payment information. This should fully detail how much postage will cost and what forms of payment the seller will take, for example, cheques, postal orders or PayPal. A good seller will complete all this information, but some do leave it out. It is always a good idea to ask how much postage will be before bidding, as unless otherwise specified, this is paid for by the winning bidder over and above their final winning bid at a rate determined by the seller.

At the top right hand side of the page is a box containing the seller's username. This is followed by a number and a percentage score which refers to the seller's feedback rating – eBay allows buyers and sellers to rate each other on how pleased they are with the other's participation in a transaction. There is the option to give positive, neutral or negative feedback. The number in brackets shows how many positive feedbacks have been given (one is subtracted for every negative received). The percentage refers to how much of the overall feedback score is positive. Sellers and buyers with excessively negative feedback should be avoided at all costs.

Within this area, there are also links allowing you to read the feedback comments left by the seller's previous trading partners, and to see the other items they are selling. You can also send off questions about the item to the seller through eBay's internal messaging system.

The very top of the page will also have a link allowing you to 'Watch' the item by adding it to your 'My eBay' page. All users get one of these, and it allows you to keep track of all your eBay activities such as buying, selling or monitoring auctions you may wish to bid on, or are bidding on.

This basic online auctioning system still holds true to its roots, working in the same way it did when the site was first launched. Items can be listed for one day, three days, five days, seven days or ten days. Sellers can set a start price of whatever amount they choose, and they also have the option of setting a reserve – a hidden amount that if not reached, means the item goes unsold.

Sellers also have the option of adding 'Buy It Now' prices, where a buyer can purchase the item immediately if they are willing to pay the amount set for it. eBay also allows 'Fixed Price Listings' whereby no bidding is involved, and the item goes to whoever clicks the 'Buy' button and agrees to pay the amount specified.

On a standard auction, bids can be entered at any time, but many people choose to 'watch' items before bidding on them at the last second. This way, they can avoid driving the price up and minimise the danger of being outbid.

Bids are made by clicking on the 'Place Bid' button. You can then enter the amount you are willing to pay – along with your username and password if you are not already logged onto the site - and click 'Bid Now'. You will then reach a page that either tells you that you are the highest bidder – you will also receive an e-mail confirming this – or that you have been outbid.

At the start of an auction, the seller will set a start price. The first bid must be for this amount or greater. Bid increments are pre-set at standard levels by eBay. These are as follows:

£0.01 – £1.00	Increment	£0.05
£1.01 – £5.00	Increment	£0.20
£5.01 – £15.00	Increment	£0.50
£15.01 – £60.00	Increment	£1.00
£60.01 – £150.00	Increment	£2.00
£150.01 – £300.00	Increment	£5.00
£300.01 – £600.00	Increment	£10.00
£600.01 – £1,500.00	Increment	£20.00
£1,500.01 – £3,000.00	Increment	£50.00
£3,000.01 – Upwards	Increment	£100.00

March 2005

Hence, if the item has been bid up to £25, the minimum you will be able to bid is £26. If it has been bid up to £69.73, then you must bid a minimum of £71.73, and so on.

If an item starts at £2, you can't place a bid lower than that starting price – but you can bid any amount above that £2. For example, you could bid £5. The auction's page will then register that one bid has been received. The price will remain at £2, unless someone else also bids – if they bid £2.20, the minimum increase on the start price, then the system will take them to a page telling them they have been outbid, and the item's price will rise to £2.40 with you still as the highest bidder.

This will continue until someone bids over your £5. If another user bids £5 exactly as well, then the price will rise to this amount, but as your bid was placed first, you will still be the highest bidder. This holds true at any point during the auction process. For example, if a £155 item has two bids and you bid the minimum of £160, then the system may take you to the 'You Have Been Outbid' page. This will be because the previous bidder entered a higher maximum bid amount. The current bid price of the item will increase to £165, but the other user will still remain the highest bidder.

Since bids can be placed right up to the last second, if you are the highest bidder, you can still be outbid at any point up until the close of the auction if someone enters a higher amount than you have. If this happens, then the system will send you an e-mail informing you that you have been outbid. You can then choose whether or not to bid again. If you do decide to bid again and win the item, then you will be sent an e-mail confirming this, as will the seller.

If the seller has specified postage costs, a 'Pay Now' button will appear on the completed auction page. If not, there will be a link for you to request the total from them, including postage. If you are buying internationally then you should do this anyway, as the postage costs specified may only be for domestic shipping, and international delivery will undoubtedly cost more. There will also be a link for the seller to send you an electronic invoice, which you will receive by e-mail.

The seller will specify what method they can be paid by; most take cheques and postal orders as well as online payment using systems like PayPal, Nochex and BidPay. Items bought on eBay are paid for in advance and are then sent out by the seller. You should also note that, unlike traditional real world auctions, eBay charges no VAT or final premium to the buyer. Once the payment and item have been received, and both buyer and seller are happy, they can leave positive feedback for each other.

If the item turns out not to be as described – or if it never actually arrives – then it is up to you to contact the seller and sort it out between you. Bear in mind that the online payment service, PayPal, has built-in protection for buyers whose sellers never send out the item. In the meantime, if the seller fails to sort out a problem to your satisfaction, you can always leave them negative or neutral feedback – although remember they can do the same for you! It is for this reason that it's a good idea to avoid sellers with excessive negative feedback.

If you should deal with someone who you feel has ripped you off, you can report him or her to eBay – anyone with very excessive amounts of negative feedback will be banned from the site. There are also mediation forums like Square Trade where buyers and sellers with disputes can be helped by a mediator to work out their differences. There is a fee for this but a successful outcome can result in agreements from both parties to withdraw negative feedback that could otherwise not be removed. Negative feedback is permanent and can only be removed if left by mistake for the wrong user, or under a few other very stringent circumstances.

It should be said, however, that those who don't abide by the eBay rules are in the minority. Most users have overwhelmingly positive feedback, and the eBay experience is usually a very satisfactory one. After all, many users have the opportunity to buy unusual and hard-to-find items, and the site has been the springboard for many international friendships.

Online Payment Methods

Back when the first internet pioneers started selling goods over the web, one of the most immediate concerns was how consumers would pay for their items. While entering credit card details into an online form may seem the simplest way of completing a transaction, the safety of having to disclose this information over the internet was, and still is, one of the biggest concerns to internet shoppers.

Initially, various different companies tried to solve the problem by creating e-currencies. Of these, the best known were Beenz and Flooz. You could earn 'beenz' or 'flooz' by visiting certain sites and taking surveys or by shopping; the idea being that commercial sites would accept these online units in lieu of cash – which they would then claim back from the Beenz or Flooz websites. In practice, however, the idea was an utter failure. Neither currency caught on – mostly because they weren't accepted widely enough, which led to both sites closing down. Flooz shut down abruptly overnight and Beenz gave its users ten days to use up all the Beenz in their account before the currency became invalid.

There are, however, three online-payment systems consumers can use which still exist and thrive.

PayPal

PayPal was created to give individuals a way to cheaply and easily accept or send credit card payments to each other, without having to be registered as a business with the card companies.

When opening an account, you simply register a credit or debit card with the PayPal site. When you want to send payment to another user, you simply fill out a form detailing their e-mail address, and the amount you want to send. This amount (less a fee) is automatically charged to your card and deposited into their online account. If they have a high street bank account registered with PayPal, they can then transfer this money into it or, alternatively, the amount can remain in the PayPal account and be used to make payments to others. Simple and quick to use, PayPal soon found favour with eBay buyers who were anxious to speed up the process of getting their items shipped and could do this by paying instantly with PayPal. Indeed, PayPal was eventually bought by eBay, becoming an integral part of the auctioning giant. It is still the market leader in its field, but has been criticised by some for charging what they see as excessive fees for receiving payments.

PayPal functions in most countries across the globe and, as well as being accepted by individuals, many smaller online retailers also accept it in payment for orders.

NOCHEX

NoChex is the UK's answer to PayPal, functioning in much the same way. Like PayPal it operates globally, but with one major difference; NoChex doesn't require you to sign up for an account in order to send cash, although recipients must have an account in order to receive it.

Credit Cards

Internet credit card fraud is far less common than was once feared, and this is thanks to encryption software.

Encryption software works by scrambling whatever data is input, and transporting it in garbled form to wherever it's going. In other words, when you type in your credit card number and hit send, the encrypting software turns it into an unrecognisable string of symbol while it travels to the seller. As soon as it arrives in their system, it is unscrambled again.

Hackers attempt to view credit cards numbers in transit by intercepting them en route to the intended recipient. If the number is encrypted, even if they manage to grab the information, they will receive nothing more useful than a nonsensical string of gibberish that could take decades to crack.

The most common encrypting technology is known as SSL, or Secure Sockets Layering. You will be able to tell if the webpage you are visiting uses this technology by looking at the URL. Regular URLs are preceded by the letters 'http'

while secure SSL URLs are preceded by 'https'.

The security status will also be shown on the status bar of your browser window. This is the bar running across the bottom of your browser. If you don't have one of these, then click on the 'View' menu, and then click on 'Status Bar' to make it viewable. If you are on a secure connection, a small padlock will appear on the lower right-hand side of the status bar.

This padlock should be in the 'closed' position. If it goes to 'open', your connection is not secure. Depending on the settings you have chosen, Windows may also offer a prompt box informing you when you are entering or leaving a secure site.

Entering credit card information on a site protected in this way is as safe, if not safer, than giving your card to a waiter or waitress in a restaurant and having them take it out of your sight to the counter while you remain at the table. You should, however, avoid entering credit or debit card information if the site is not secure, as this will be fair game for any lurking hacker.

While the fear of having credit card information stolen has now receded among savvy internet users, those same long-time surfers have also become very aware of another online issue – that of privacy.

While the internet has brought many benefits, it has also brought many new forms of annoyance, the most pertinent of these being spyware and spam.

Spam is not just a variety of tinned meat. It is also the online version of junk mail, sent to your e-mail inbox instead of coming through your letterbox. Spam is sent to e-mail addresses harvested from across the internet, including from online retailers, and it can reach ridiculous levels with several hundred e-mails arriving daily.

Stopping it can be far harder than triggering it as well. Most spam messages include information on how to unsubscribe from their lists, but since many spammers share e-mail lists, the chances are that by clicking that link you have confirmed your address is active so no sooner have you unsubscribed from one spam list, another ten will start e-mailing you.

Spyware is even more malicious. It downloads itself secretly to your computer while you're visiting a website or opening an e-mail. While viruses behave in a similar way, they are designed to cause damage. Spyware is designed to simply track where you go online and send an amazing array of details about your web surfing habits back to its parent company who then use this data in market research. The trouble with spyware is that, unlike spam, you can sometimes be unaware of its presence – and while you can just delete spam, you won't even know that spyware is profiling your every move unless you check. In order to get rid of it, it's a wise idea to install an anti-spyware program, such as AdAware or SpyBot, and run it regularly to make sure no spyware is operating on your computer.

There's also a fine line between spyware and the methods of customer tracking used by most major retail websites. All of these collect data on their customers, tracking everything from what products you look at, what you order, and using this information to populate "if you liked this product, you may also like..." lists at the sides of pages, generating them more revenue. It is for similar reasons that many of these sites operate 'accounts' for users – if you get a personal welcome as you sign back into your account, it adds a 'personal touch,' hopefully making you feel like spending more money. It makes it easier to track everything you do on their site, too.

In order to minimise the annoyance and intrusion of your online privacy, here are a few steps to follow:

Beware of where you enter your details

You may think you'll enjoy a regular newsletter on a certain subject, but before you sign up for anything that requires an e-mail address, or any other contact info, read their privacy policy and make sure the information doesn't go any further. Chances are it will, and you'll regret it as you end up with countless e mails offering more 'special offers'. from a spam e-mail – this will only accelerate the cycle.

Read privacy policies

Whenever you are offered the chance to view a site's privacy policy, read it.

Sites should always display it online, especially when asking for your details, although with some of the shadier ones, you may have to ask to see it. It should state whether or not they give (or sell) your information to third (or fourth, or fifth) parties. If they do, then surf on by and don't give them your custom.

Check (or Uncheck) the opt-in/out boxes

When you enter your contact information, many sites now have little disclaimers asking if it's okay for them to contact you with other offers or information, or if it's okay for their 'affiliates' to do so as well.

Read what it says carefully – some will require you to tick a check box (or two) in order to opt out of receiving this stuff. Some will require you to uncheck the box.

Do whichever stops you from receiving this junk – you won't want it.

Fill out forms with the minimum of information

Give out as little information as possible. Some websites will have 'optional surveys' for you to complete, which ask all about your marital status, yearly income, etc. All of this is pure market research and doesn't need to be completed in order for your purchase to be processed. All the required fields that you absolutely need to fill out will either be marked with an asterisk, in a different font, or in a different colour. That's all they need to know, so that's all you need give them.

Check for TRUST UK or TRUSTe membership

TRUST UK (England) and TRUSTe (US) are independent, non-profit organisations that legitimate sites can sign up to. Member sites should display the TRUST logos prominently, and should adhere to these organisations' guidelines on protecting privacy. Any which violate these guidelines can be reported to the organisation monitors.

CAN YOU GET BARGAINS ON THE INTERNET?

For all the net's convenience and speed, the question that lingers at the back of any newcomer's mind is – will buying online actually save me money? In a lot of cases, the answer is yes. You'll need to do some surfing and comparing of price tags, but with most items, you'll find yourself paying vastly less than you would do on the high street – even when you figure in the cost of delivery.

Bargain prices are everywhere on the net. Among the items you can buy online at cut-down prices are electrical goods, books, CDs, DVDs, financial products; oh, and did we mention credit cards, bank accounts and mortgages, travel tickets, clothes, collectibles and novelty items? It's a stock list you can't find anywhere else, and all these bargains can be found both at online retailers and at auctions; the trick is to know how to find them.

By comparing the prices of many online shops with those of their real world counterparts, you may wonder how the cyber-retailers can get their price tags down so low. The answer is simple; an online retailer doesn't have the overheads associated with obtaining and maintaining shop premises; the high rents, power bills and the need to keep remodelling shop windows etc. After all, renting warehouse space to store stock, hiring processors to process orders and running a website comes in a lot cheaper. With lower overheads, prices come down, sales volume goes up, and the result is a win-win situation for all concerned.

Some online pricing trends do, however, mirror their real life counterparts. For example, the bigger online retailers are often likely to have the cheapest prices, since they can pile it high and sell it cheap. And even if they don't have the cheapest purchase prices, they may offer the cheapest shipping options – after all, if they ship very large amounts of stock, they'll be able to negotiate lower postage rates with whichever courier service they use. This can often result in many big retailers providing free delivery, which is a real bonus for the consumer. There are also seasonal sales at many retail websites, most notably right after Christmas. And many websites offer year-round special deals, just like regular shops.

 Always use comparison shopping

Whatever it is you're shopping for online, there are a few basic guidelines to follow to make sure that you get the best bargain possible. First of all, you'll want to compare as many prices as possible for the item you're looking at – especially if it's a high value product. And while you'll probably be surprised at how much cheaper some things are on the net than they are at real world shops, you're likely to be equally surprised at how much internet prices can vary from seller to seller.

Just like in real life, you wouldn't think of buying a washing machine, computer, car or any other similar item from the first place you went into, would you? Well, one of the best things about shopping online is that browsing from the comfort of your own home makes it much easier to comparison shop for the best prices.

While in real life, this can often involve trudging round numerous places, going online means it can all be done with a few clicks of the mouse. And best of all, it can even be done with smaller items. If you're looking for a certain DVD or CD in a real world shop, savings can be so minimal between stores that often you may not even bother shopping around. The ease, though, with which comparing can be done on the internet, means that you can look properly and make those vital savings. Remember the old adage about taking care of the pennies? It might be a cliché, but it certainly holds true online.

The easiest way to comparison shop online is to simply type in the URLs of as many different online shops as you want, and search their sites for the product you're looking for. Note down the prices (and any extras you'll have to pay on top) and go for whoever offers the best deal. Auctions will be covered in more detail later, but if you're happy buying something second-hand, then do check those out too, as you may well find that desirable item for cheaper. But how do you go about comparing prices online if you only know

one online store or, worse still, don't know any at all? It's best to use comparison-shopping agents that take the hassle out of finding items and retailers.

Acting like a search engine, these sites allow you to enter a product name and search for it. The engine will then bring up all the sites it can find which sell that particular item, and will give comparable details of all their prices, shipping costs etc. Thus you can quickly sift through the results and see at a glance which online stores are cheapest. Many of these comparison agents are specialist in nature with some searching DVD and CD retailers, while others search prices on computers or electrical items. Some agents will also give you consumer reviews of products.

When using a comparison agent, however, do be mindful of two things. Firstly, the agent may have one or more 'partner sites' whose results will come up either in front of the results from other sites, or in a bolder colour. These won't always be the best deals; they'll just be the sites that have given the comparison agent a cut of their takings or some advertising revenue – so do make sure you read all the results.

Also bear in mind that agents sometimes search out products that are either no longer for sale or have been discontinued, or which are on websites that are no longer functioning. So, when you do come across an item you like, always check the particular site to see whether the item is still on sale at that price, and that you can still place an order.

While many comparison agents give users the opportunity to rate or write reviews of products, there are other sites solely dedicated to this purpose. These allow surfers to write about their experiences with a product, and some have ratings systems as well. These sites exist for almost every conceivable product – from cars and software to computers and everything in between. Often, the information here can be invaluable as it isn't processed magazine reviewing where the reviewer only had the product for a short period of time; these are reviews from fellow consumers who have had day-to-day use of an item. Taking the time to read a few of these reviews may help you avoid items that are plagued with problems in everyday life, and even help point you in the direction of a hassle-free alternative.

When using a comparison agent, always remember that you will be buying from an independent retailer, and not from the agent itself. While the agent can find you a great bargain, how do you know if the retailer itself is reputable?

Make sure retailers are reputable

Checking that a retailer is reputable is a must, no matter how you came across them. If you're buying from a well-known online retailer such as Amazon or through the website of well-known real life store, then it's pretty much guaranteed that you're buying from a reputable seller – and if you do have a problem with your purchase, you'll know where to go, what to do, and that your complaint will be dealt with.

If, however, you're buying from a smaller, less well-known seller, you may be less certain of their reputation. Fret not though because there are certain steps you can – and should – take to protect yourself. Firstly, search the site and find a physical address that the company is registered at, so you'll know where to contact them. Another tip is to look for a customer services number and then call it to make sure it works. Just make sure you check that it's not a premium-rate number before doing so!

It may also be worth searching for the company's name on any popular search engine and checking to see if anybody has been posting negative comments about the retailer online. With the world wide web as extensive as it is now, it's virtually impossible to rip people off without them taking to the message boards to give the company in question a bashing.

Do also ensure that the company's purchasing pages are securely encrypted, by checking for all the details we noted in the earlier section about online security. If they aren't, then don't buy from that site – no matter how cheap the prices are.

Oh, and while you can sometimes take poorly written descriptions and missing information as signs of a dodgy website, this isn't always the case. Some of the biggest retailers in the UK have been known to make mistakes like these on their sites, and yet they are still safe enough to buy from.

 Watch out for additional costs

Another thing to look out for are add-on costs. It's a given when shopping remotely, whether it's online or through a printed catalogue, that any item you purchase will have to be sent to you. But you may well have to pay for this on top of the purchase price of your item, and if you're bargain hunting, you'll need to take care that shipping costs don't wipe out your saving.

Most retail websites offer a variety of shipping options, with the general rule being that the more expensive the shipping is, the faster the item or items will reach you. If delivery speed is of the essence, you'll likely find yourself paying extra for the convenience.

If you're making multiple purchases at the same time and not all

the items you've ordered are in stock, some websites also offer the option of having your order held until all items are in their warehouse and ready to be shipped. Alternatively, you can opt to have the items sent to you individually as and when they are available. Often, this will affect the delivery costs, as you may find yourself paying two (or more) sets of postage and packing charges, depending on how many parcels your order is shipped in.

To get the cheapest delivery, your best option will likely be to opt for the slowest method, and for all your items to be combined into one delivery. Often, as long as the items are shipped from an inland address, the longest delivery time will still not be more than a week – although you should check and note delivery times down when placing your order. If the items don't arrive within the allotted time frame, they may need to be chased up, and it's never a good idea to leave this too long.

If you're buying from the online outlet of a real world store, you may also want to check if you can collect the item from a branch close to you, as this may make things even cheaper – especially with large items like kitchen appliances or other household electrics.

If you are ordering from abroad, then make sure you go over the shipping costs with a fine toothcomb, as it's likely to be expensive, especially if the item is sent with any sort of insured service. With some sellers, however, such insurance may be optional and sometimes, retailers shipping internationally will send items by surface mail instead of by air, which is much cheaper.

Do bear in mind though that it can take an extremely long time for items to arrive by sea, and insurance may not be available on this option. If you do go for surface mail or waive the option of insurance on airmail, you may have to sign something stating that the shipping is at your own risk, and that the seller is indemnified against any sort of claim should the item not arrive.

If you are shopping on a US website, you should remember that prices will exclude sales tax. In American shops, this is added at the cash register, and in the same way, many US websites will charge it when orders are processed. US sales tax should, however, only be applicable to items sold to US buyers. If you're having an item sent outside of America, then you should get it tax-free. Some US websites will be aware of this – usually the ones who do a lot of international business; others though won't be and may charge you sales tax anyway.

If you are considering buying from an American site, read the 'Frequently Asked Questions' section to clarify their tax status and international shipping options – as some won't sell internationally, especially those that are online versions of real world shops. If their position is not clearly stated, e-mail their customer services and ask for more information.

The exchange rates can also make buying from abroad an

attractive proposition, but it's always better to be safe than sorry by calculating the added costs first before going ahead with a purchase. Also, do watch out for some domestic UK websites that sneakily don't include the VAT in their advertised prices for VAT-applicable items – although they should state clearly that it isn't included in the prices as given. VAT is 17.5%, so if the item is subject to it, then note whether it's included and, if it isn't, add it on to the shipping costs.

Pay by credit card – or use an online payment system

Ironically, while many consumers were initially worried about their credit details being stolen from online transactions, in many ways you're actually safer using a credit card to make purchases on the internet because most will protect you should the goods not arrive, or not arrive in the condition they were expected.

If you buy online, be it from a small retailer or an individual on eBay, you should never send cash, and please avoid paying by cheque if you can pay by credit or debit card. The reason for this is simple; most credit cards cover you for fraudulent transactions i.e. if you do find that you've been scammed and can't get anywhere with the seller (or if they turn out to be fictitious), you can complain to the card company.

With a small deductible, often set at £50, most credit cards carry purchase protection, and you can claim back fraudulent charges from them. Some may even cover you for the whole amount, and many debit cards have the same protection levels. Cheques and, worst of all, cash, have no built-in protection.

Bearing this in mind, it's a good idea to check with the literature that came with your card as to what sort of protection the credit card company offers for online purchases. You may find that it

doesn't offer any (some cards do not) but if you do intend to shop online regularly, you might want to shop around for a different card that offers you proper protection.

PayPal and other online payment systems also have buyer protection measures. On PayPal, for example, if an item paid for doesn't arrive, then their claims process allows you to lodge a complaint against the seller. If they cannot prove that they have shipped the item by giving you a tracking number for the shipment, then they must refund your money.

Complaints can also be lodged in other instances, like the items not matching their description or being in a poorer-than-advertised condition. If you're a seller, do also note that in many complaint procedures, online payment services will usually find in favour of the bidder, so take steps to protect yourself against the more unscrupulous buyers out there.

Look for online specials

Very often, retailers will use their websites to advertise run-out or refurbished items that they need to shift, and such deals can provide substantial savings. Run-out items are products that are being replaced with new models, and therefore retailers need to get rid of them quickly. With so many consumers now scoping out potential purchases online before buying, websites are the perfect place to advertise items like these. The advertising costs are minimal which is good news for the companies who want to spend most of their ad budgets on new, higher-priced items.

Run-out items are very often advertised on website front pages, as this is the page that most people are likely to hit first. This gives the run-out items maximum exposure, and ensures that consumers will think the entire website will be full of similar bargains. Other popular sellers on the internet are refurbished items. These are products that have been previously used, but which have then been serviced and had any faults rectified by experts. They are usually electrical items and are often sold online by electrical shops that have a real world presence, or direct from manufacturer websites. In most cases, refurbished products come with warranties comparable to their equivalent new counterparts – although you should check this before you buy – but will be considerably cheaper to purchase.

If you are thinking of going the refurbished route, though, only buy from a reputable dealer. Also, check the specs of whatever item it is you're interested in to make sure they're up to standard, and that the price matches these specs.

Watch out for items which can differ to pictures

As we've said, many websites now do far more than just offer a small picture of the item you're considering buying; they have pop-up high-resolution pictures, downloadable films and other flash promos to grab your wallet's attention. And while products like electrical goods don't differ much in appearance from their online photographs, some items can look very different in pictures from the way they do in real life. Colours can vary greatly between a computer monitor and reality, while the size of large items needs to be checked very carefully to make sure you aren't getting a distorted view of its real size. As we've pointed out, these factors can particularly affect clothes and furnishings.

When shopping for such items online, check return policies very carefully before you part with your cash. Shopping with a credit card may provide extra consumer protection, but making claims on a card for a small item can be time-consuming and annoying to deal with, and may ultimately not be worth it.

After you've checked to see what return policies the seller has, take full advantage of whatever features the website has in order to get the best look at an item before you buy. If possible, try to view a picture of a clothing item actually being worn to see how the colours contrast with skin tone, and how the piece hangs. And look for pictures of that furniture actually in room settings, so you can compare it in size to other furniture items; nothing can be more disorienting than a picture of a couch, table or sideboard floating on a white background. Note down the measurements given too, and check these on a tape measure to get a better idea of size.

As stated, you'll find that most large websites will have good pictures of their products, but one area where you may find that the images are rather lacking in quality is at online auctions. It's a fact that online auctions that don't feature pictures of the item on offer, rarely sell well – in fact, often they won't sell at all. Sadly, not all sellers understand the need for good pictures and not all have the capability, either technically or artistically, to take them.

As a result, you may well find yourself browsing through out-of-focus and blurry images of goods that have been taken using low-pixel digital cameras, or mobile phone-cams. If this is the case, ask for more pictures to be sent to you by e-mail before the auction ends. Either that, or ask the seller to describe in fuller detail any particular wear or damage to the item which you might be worried about – the 'ask seller a question' button is there for a reason. And if you don't use the option before the end, and the item does arrive damaged, the seller may well have recourse to refuse a refund by simply saying that you didn't ask before the auction ended.

Finding bargains at auction on the internet

Mention the words 'online auction' and most people will associate the phrase with eBay such is its popularity. Hence, most of the tricks and tips included here are aimed at eBay or similar sites. However, there are a few other sites that also run auctions, using a slightly different format. These are specialist sites usually dedicated to selling one sort of item such as computers, for example, or one particular type of antique. These adhere to the more traditional form of an auction, charging the buyer premiums and storage fees for items not collected etc.

The best advice for using one of these sites is to make yourself aware of all the costs before you buy – and, most importantly, to know your subject – as these sites generally won't be equipped for bidders to ask questions about the merchandise prior to the end of the sale. And again, as with a real-life auction, know the value of the items concerned, and don't bid more than you can afford to – or want to – in order to buy them.

Not bidding more than you can afford is also important. It is very easy to get caught up in the bidding momentum and wind up paying far too much for an item, often exceeding its actual value in the process – and going over your pre-decided limit. Such is the gambling aspect of online auctions that you can often forget that you're bidding with real money.

When shopping on an auction site, keep a cool head at all times, even when things get crazy in the last few minutes of the auction, and the pressure might lead you into getting carried away. Hold firmly on to those purse strings during such moments, or your bank account could end up regretting your hot-headedness.

Such temptation though is the nature of the beast. After all, it didn't take long for savvy eBayers to figure out that the best bidding strategy for winning items at the lowest prices, is to bid as late as possible. Whether the seller has chosen the one, three, five, seven or ten day auction option, you'll generally find that not a lot of bidding happens until the last day. This is because bidding earlier is seen as simply driving the price up, and leaving yourself wide open to being outbid. Hence, he who bids at the last second has a better chance of winning, since there will be no time left for other bidders to enter the picture. And as internet connections get faster, bidding can get closer and closer – sometimes down to the last split second.

One bidder we spoke to told us that he had refreshed the auction page at the point where there were 'zero seconds' left to bid. He was, of course, expecting to see that his bid had won the day. Unfortunately, when he reloaded the page to see the final standings, he was dismayed to see that his bid had been bettered at the last millisecond. Bidding strategies like these can often see item prices doubling in the last minute too, so if you do bid early, you will want to set as high a maximum bid as possible. Although, unless it's an item that absolutely nobody else wants, this is unlikely to net you a bargain.

Even of you do lose out, don't worry too much because nine times out of ten, a similar product will pop up. The best way to track them down is by using the service's search engine. To find the maximum number of items, you'll want to search internationally within both heading and body text.

Not only will this return the maximum number of auctions for you to browse through, but it may also help you grab a bargain, especially if what you're looking for is a small collectable, or similar item. Often, people list a lot of similar items, and the thing you're looking for may be included in one of these, but will only be mentioned by name in the body text, and not in the actual heading.

Also, don't be put off by the idea of buying more than you initially wanted to in one auction – buying a large lot and then selling the unwanted items off can often end up working out cheaper than buying a single item. In some cases, it may even wind up making you a profit.

Searching internationally means you'll get a wider variety of items to choose from. Some items may well be cheaper in other countries, and some collectibles may have far more availability and be cheaper in other parts of the world. Exchange rates can also work in your favour, but remember that international shipping can be expensive, so check the cost of this before deciding to bid – especially if the item is large or heavy.

You may also need to take into consideration that if you are UK-based and are buying from outside the EU, the seller will be required to attach a customs label declaring the value of the

contents. If the item's value exceeds £18, including the postage, you'll end up paying import duties on top of the purchase price and the shipping charges.

For the cunning bargain hunters among you, it's worthwhile looking for common misspellings of items or brand names – why? Well, very often, people mistype the names of items when they're writing the auction text, or simply don't check to see if they have spelt their text correctly. But on eBay, such a simple (or sloppy) mistake can be a seller's undoing.

Remember, eBay is a search engine-based site, and the site's strongest selling items are invariably brand names. People often want labels, and because the item is branded, they are easier to find because they have specific names to search for. However, if that brand name is typed wrongly, then far fewer searchers will find the item, and it will most likely attract fewer bids. This can mean that the item ends up going cheaper and prove to be the best bargain.

Seller misspellings do, by the way, give rise to the one instance where it can be a good idea to bid early. If the opening bid is low enough, and the seller has misspelt an important word in the title, then make your opening bid as soon as you find the auction. This is a rather sneaky tactic because eBay's rules dictate that the seller can only alter the wording of an auction title or its text if it has no bids. But once the first bid is placed, both the title and the text are locked. All the seller can then do is merely add to the text.

So, by bidding, you will prevent the seller from being able to alter the misspelt headline, even if they become aware of the mistake. Mind you, if there is less than a day to go on the auction, they can still end it early without selling to the highest bidder but few will do this because of the hassle involved.

While you're running those searches for common mistakes, don't just look for misspellings – look up variations on the name of whatever you're looking for. Try abbreviations, slang names or generic item names. These may well turn up additional items. If you've got time to kill, then try a few off-the-wall ideas, as people may sometimes not know what they're selling and will try

describing it in a 'humorous' way. You can also use such methods when browsing items by category – after all, it's not uncommon for a seller to put their item in a similar but incorrect category.

Lastly, do take the odd risk. While not all risks will pay off, some undoubtedly will. Certain items just don't sell on eBay because they aren't products that have a market on such a site. These include paintings by unknown artists, unbranded jewellery and wedding dresses.

This may be because of the way these items are presented in their pictures, or because it's hard to list them so people can find them – or perhaps they're just not items that buyers feel comfortable with buying online. However, even if you weren't considering buying such items at an online auction, it may well be worth going for it – after all, if the price is low enough, even if it does turn out to be a dud, your bank balance won't have suffered too much, and you never know – you might well come out ahead.

SHOPPING ONLINE FOR SPECIFIC BARGAINS

Here we take a look at some of the most popular products sought-after by online shoppers.

 Collectibles & antiques

In no small way, eBay has revolutionised the marketplace for small antiques and collectibles, most particularly anything of suitable size for sending through the post. It's made life easier for collectors, who previously would have had to wait for specialist fairs to come to town, or force them to visit antique markets miles away. Another advantage is that eBay has given sellers access to a far wider market than they ever had before, and for buyers, the auction site has opened up possibilities for collecting items that barely existed before.

But this is not the only online resource for collectors. Go to any search engine and start browsing for information on whatever item it is that you collect, and you can be almost guaranteed to find that someone has set up a website about it, and that web discussion forums have been created to discuss it. Joining these can be a fantastic source of information, advice and friendship, as collectors can swap items and arrange sales through them, as well as share information. These can be particularly helpful if you are interested in a type of item that's rare in your own country, but common abroad.

There are also plenty of antique shops that sell their stock online by mail order. Prices will probably be commensurate with going market rates, but for finding that elusive item that can't be sourced closer to home, using the net may be the answer. However, unless you find a message board buddy willing to sell cheap or swap for something you've already got, then you'll invariably wind back up at eBay.

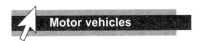

Motor vehicles

Buying a car online has never been easier. Manufacturer websites now often assist you in pricing a car, searching out a financing deal and completing the whole buying process in the minimum amount of time. You can also shop at eBay for real cars just as easily as you can for toy ones – and find some real bargains in the process.

So successful has the world's premier auction site been at selling full-size vehicles, that eBay US now has eBay Motors, a separate site dedicated to just selling cars, trucks, vans and all other things automotive. In the UK, cars are still listed on the regular eBay site, but its popularity as an effective way to shift your motor is growing daily.

Vehicles that go up for sale at online auctions are often there because owners want a quick, painless way to get rid of them without the hassle of having them stuck in the drive for months while they're advertised in online classifieds. If they're really keen to sell, the seller may even put the car up for auction with no reserve price.

Nevertheless, there's always a real risk that the remote nature of internet auctioning is being used to dispose of a car which has serious problems. If you are thinking of buying a vehicle at an online auction, you should always read the description thoroughly, and then contact the seller in advance to ask further questions about it.

If you're still interested, go and examine the vehicle as you would any other used car you were considering buying. You may want to pay a professional to carry out mechanical checks, and it's also a good idea to pay for an HPI check, which ensures that the vehicle isn't stolen or a write-off. Any genuine owner shouldn't have a problem with you wanting to carry out such safety measures. If they do, then forget bidding on their auction – better to be safe than sorry, especially with a purchase the size of a car, and with its potential to wreak financial havoc if something expensive goes wrong with it.

Besides auctions and dealers, you'll also find a lot of sites with online classifieds for cars and many other products. Browsing these should yield lots of possibilities, although they needn't be any better than those you'd find in similar publications offline. You'll generally have to pay for access to the websites of dedicated classified ad publications as well, so it may not work out any cheaper than buying the ads paper or magazine; but do bear in mind that some sites update their online classifieds on a daily basis.

If you're after a classic car or specialist vehicle that has one or more owners' clubs, then you should take a look at the club websites. Many of these have their own classifieds with vehicles for sale, and often they are free to browse. The same goes for specialist mechanics who cater for particular makes or models. If they have websites, they often advertise cars for sale there.

If, on the other hand, you're looking for a new vehicle and want to save some cash, you may want to consider one of the online agencies specialising in importing cars from abroad. Since the 1990s, much has been written about how vastly car prices differ from country to country within Europe, and about how much can potentially be saved by buying your car in a country where the same model is cheaper to buy than in your homeland.

Comparing prices of cars in various different countries is fairly easy – a quick trip to your favourite search engine should give you access to numerous websites offering price comparisons between various countries. From there, it should be plain sailing too; all you theoretically have to do is go to the manufacturer's website, locate a dealer in the country of your choice, and order through them over the phone.

Mainland European dealers can't legally refuse to sell you a right-hand-drive car, but in many cases, you may have to overcome a language barrier and the actual ordering can be a fraught business. You also need to figure in the cost of your international phone calls and of travelling to whichever country you are collecting your vehicle from. Since this can all be tricky and time-consuming, numerous agencies have sprung up offering to take the hassle out of the whole process by doing it for you – for a fee. Initially, these agencies used to simply advertise in the backs of car magazines, but most now have websites.

If you are considering buying a car through an agency, you'll need to keep a handle on all aspects of the process to ensure that you don't wind up seriously out of pocket. To start with, if you do decide to go through an agency, you'll need to check that they're legitimate.

This sort of business is ideal for con artists, as it involves large sums of money and up-front payments. So try to use an agent that's been recommended by someone you know, or check online to see if there are any horror stories linked to your favoured agent.

You should also consider whether using an agency is actually worth it. If you speak a European language and don't mind doing all the legwork yourself – and have the spare time – then you can simply bypass agency fees. Such fees are likely to far outweigh the cost of phone calls and a plane ticket to collect your car - especially if you book a cheap flight online!

Whether you decide to go through an agency, or sort it all out yourself, don't forget that you'll need to pay VAT on the car. It may well be cheaper to do this once you get the car back to the UK – contact the customs and excise department for full details on how to do this by visiting their website at www.hmce.gov.uk. You'll also need to check with the DVLA about getting temporary insurance for your car until you can have it registered on UK plates.

Buying a car from abroad isn't confined to Europe though – there are now agencies that sell Japanese-market 'grey import' second-hand cars. Cars sourced from Japan are often desirable performance and luxury models that are unavailable outside their home market. However, the Japanese MOT test is so hard to pass and expensive to take that it renders most three-year-old vehicles virtually obsolete and valueless, even though they may still be in excellent condition.

As the vehicles are right-hand-drive, many importers in countries like England, Australia and Africa (which also drive on the left), saw a gap in the market and began buying and importing these vehicles, then selling them on.

Many agencies specialising in these vehicles can be found online, and they differ from agencies which can get you a new European vehicle, in that most have actually already bought the cars they're selling, and will either have them in storage in the UK or en route from Japan. If you are looking for a particular model or specification though, many can source you a car that matches your needs too.

Again, it is possible to buy from Japan yourself; many of the cars these importers buy are sold at auction, and Japanese auctioneers also have online auctions for their cars. You will, however, then have to sort out your own shipping and deal with modifying the vehicle for UK roads. Many of these cars require alterations to the lights and other items before they can be legally registered in the UK.

Still more agencies based online specialise in supplying American cars, which are also home-market only. These include sports and luxury cars, four-wheel drives and vehicles such as stretch limousines, which are used for business. Again, these cars may need modifications to make them legal for British road use, and the advantage of going through an agency is that they can take care of this for you.

You will, however, pay more than the average American consumer for your car, as the agency will charge you a fee to cover the VAT, conversions and their cut of the deal – although the car's rarity in the UK may well offset this cost. Do remember, though, that the

car will still be left-hand-drive, as right-hand-drive conversions may be very expensive or simply impossible.

If you do have your heart set on a Ford Mustang, it's worth checking out eBay Motors too. Often, US dealers use the site to sell new cars with warranties, so it's perfectly possible to buy from one of them, arrange your own shipping, and deal with the VAT while making sure the car is road-legal.

Clothing

If you're looking for fashion bargains, there are two things you ought to try. First of all, surf by some online outlet shops, which sell a huge variety of items, from sportswear and designer dresses to children's clothing, and all at reasonable prices. There are an especially large number of children's clothing specialists, which can be an absolute godsend for parents tired of paying a fortune keeping their fast-growing offspring in trendy clothes. Many of these outlets can be found through your favourite price-comparison search engine by searching for the designer or manufacturer's name.

To ensure that you are getting a bargain, check the place is legitimate and read the returns policy carefully, since you won't be able to try before you buy. Make sure you are getting a bargain by comparing the prices of their items to the prices of similar items in other shops too. It's easy enough to blind you with HTML graphics claiming low prices – but in reality, such claims might turn out to be somewhat exaggerated. And again, make sure you examine the super-sized pictures of everything and know what colour you're ordering, since colours can vary from computer screen to real life.

Don't forget eBay, of course – after all, designer clothing is one

of the site's biggest sellers. But as most of it is used, you'll need to tread cautiously when buying. Ask extra questions – like specific measurements if you aren't sure whether a particular size will fit you. And if shopping from abroad, remember that sizes in Europe, the UK and the US are all different. If the item

you're buying is a designer good, then you should pay through an online payment system – there are plenty of excellent fakes out there, and you don't want to get ripped off.

As soon as the item arrives, examine it for authenticity and if in doubt, take it to the manufacturer's shop and ask the staff there if it is authentic. If it isn't, then you'll be able to use the online payment system's safety mechanisms to get your money back, even if the seller has a no-refund policy.

Finally, you'll discover that the internet is a brilliant source for the wackiest theme clothing money can buy. Sweatshirts, underwear and even t-shirts with slogans and logos about pop-culture, politics and the like, are all available online – and it's highly unlikely you'll find some of these in the real world. Prices are generally reasonable and many favourite sites, particularly humour-based ones, will sell their own t-shirts as a sideline. These can be fantastic fun and ideal for making a statement.

 Computers, accessories & software

Computers are another top-seller on eBay, but another item that you'll need to exercise extreme caution when buying. While many computer sellers are genuine people wanting to sell machines they no longer use but that are still in good working order, there are other sellers who may simply be trying to offload a dodgy system. So, be sure to check feedback ratings, ask questions, and, as always, pay by an online system.

You'll also find numerous business-sellers using eBay to sell computers and related equipment, including just-obsolete or refurbished items. These can be fantastic value, but, again, check their feedback to make sure they're on the level and have plenty of satisfied customers. eBay is also the essential place to buy such products as USB cords and broadband phone line filters, as the prices here will be the absolute cheapest you'll find anywhere.

Should you be in the market for a refurbished computer with a guarantee, check manufacturer websites with online shops, or the big electrical retailers, as they may well have such items for sale. There may also be fantastic bargains to be had on run-out models, and these do come up often because technology moves fast these days.

All the major electrical retailers, and smaller retailers, sell computers and accessories online. Again, use one of the comparison search engines to find yourself the best bargain if you know which model of computer you want.

If you travel regularly, or have friends abroad, consider buying from overseas, especially from the US. The exchange rate and lower price tags there can make computers excellent bargain-buys. Laptops are especially tempting because they can be easily bought and brought back in your luggage. You can also try buying on eBay from US retailers if they ship worldwide, but you will find that the US equivalents of our high street electrical retailers will block attempts to buy online from abroad.

Computers are, of course, not much good without the software to run on them. Many retailers stock software, and, in a lot of cases, they'll let you download it directly to your computer, which saves on storage space and the annoyance of having to wait for the package to arrive in the post; not to mention the delivery costs. It's also worth paying a visit to the particular program's homepage if it has one, or the maker's website if not. Often you'll be able to find free trial versions of software, especially if what you're looking for is a recent release. In many cases, you'll get the complete versions of the software for free, for anything from a couple of days up to a year or longer.

Before spending any money on software, you should also make sure that you do actually need to pay for it – freeware, for example, is software that is distributed free of charge. In many cases though, there will be several versions of a particular program produced; one with more features than the others. The complete version will be the one you have to pay for while the others will be free to download. But often you'll find that you don't need all the applications for casual use, and the free version will suit your needs perfectly.

Entertainment

It could be argued that shopping on the internet is a form of entertainment in itself. However, all the traditional forms of entertainment – books, music, cinema and theatre tickets – are available online, and it's never been easier to book tickets for plays, movies and concerts using the internet. Many ticket-sellers, including cinema chains, now also offer loyalty cards that entitle you to money off.

When it comes to in-demand, one-off events like concerts and new plays though, it's a good idea to use the internet to visit as many relevant sites as possible to check when event tickets are likely to go on sale. Then you should buy over the net immediately they become available at a recognised venue such as Ticketmaster, to avoid paying vastly inflated sums to indepen-

dent agencies at a later date when the tickets are all 'sold out'.

Numerous services are available online to let you download music and even films legally, and at a reasonable cost. But if you prefer your movies to come on a DVD, then try Netflix or a similar DVD-rental-by-post operation. Once you've paid your subscription fee, you can select the movies you want to see and add them to your online list. These will then be mailed to you one at a time in the order you put them on your list, and come with a pre-paid envelope for their postal return. You can keep them as long as you like with no late fees, and the next film on your list is sent to you as soon as you return the last.

If, on the other hand, you prefer to buy DVDs and CDs, there are plenty of comparison search engines out there that can scour online retailers for the best prices. This is especially a good idea to try when you're looking for expensive box sets of movies, TV shows or music. Alternatively, go second-hand and buy on eBay. Often you'll find massive savings on pre-owned items, and you can always sell them on once you get bored with them. eBay is also an excellent source of rarer movies and music, including vinyl and videotape formats.

Utility services

Most power, gas, electricity and telephone companies now have online bill payment and account management systems that can make life a lot easier. But using the internet is also a great way to look at the sites of rival suppliers to check out their prices. Often, if you decide to switch suppliers, you can do so online too, making it all quick, easy and painless – and there may be bonuses for new customers who sign up using the company's website.

If it's a telephone or internet service you're looking for, the same benefits can apply. A good tip here is to seek out smaller companies, especially with internet service providers, as they may well be able to undercut their larger rivals in terms of price and services.

Finally, if it's a mobile phone contract you're after, the net is a fantastic place to look for deals. Most providers advertise excellent online-only specials with free extras or snappy phones thrown in as part of the deal. Always check the retailers' actual websites though, as they may well not have details of such offers in their real world shops. You can usually buy over the phone too, if you don't want to actually purchase online.

Financial products and services

American banks were among the very first service-providing institutions to offer online services and internet banking has since become a massive time and money saver for many people. All the high street banks, lenders, credit card companies and mortgage providers have websites, where you can find full details of their accounts, interest rates, free-balance transfers and more. Even better are the many financial advice sites that offer comparison tables showing which of institutions offer the best (and worst) deals.

The past few years have seen the arrival of numerous online-only banks too, and these can provide a fantastic alternative to high street names. As they have no physical branches costs are cut and in many cases, the interest paid on customer accounts is higher. There are no limits on ATMs, either, as cards can be used through the Link system, or in any participating ATM machine. Often these are also 'ethical' companies, which don't invest in countries where people or the environment are being exploited.

 Furniture & household goods

Like designer clothing labels, you'll now find that all the major furniture designers and shops have websites, some of which you can order items through. As with clothes though, care does needs to be taken when buying furniture online. We've already talked about how colours and textures can differ between a computer monitor and reality, but that potential problem applies even more so here, as many furniture items are expensive and complex to return.

Checking item sizes is therefore essential – after all, pictures on a screen can be distorting and misleading, intentionally or otherwise. With large items, check the cost of delivery carefully as well – you may still be able to get free delivery, but in most cases you'll need to pay and you generally won't be able to collect the items from a physical shop, either. If you do have the option to collect directly from the shop, then you may discover that simply buying from a real world store could actually be cheaper – so, do your research.

The same principles also apply to household electrical items, but you may find online-only specials that make the cost of delivery worthwhile. So, if you're in the market for a fridge, freezer or washing machine, make sure you browse all the major retailer sites and check for the best prices through price-comparison search engines.

eBay is also a source of furniture, as well as smaller household items. Designer sofas, suites, chairs, tables and their ilk sell very well and can be found at extremely good prices. However, if possible, it really is a good idea to view items like this before you buy, as seller pictures can be inadequate or misleading.

Verifying the condition yourself can make the difference between a bargain and disappointment when it comes to second-hand furniture. You'll also need to take the collection/delivery issue into account; if the seller is very far away, buying a cheap, commonly-found item may not be worth bothering with, as transport costs are likely to far outstrip the original purchase price.

Some sellers may deliver, if they have the capability, but will very likely charge for this. Second-hand household electrics also sell on eBay, but as with all used electrical items, they should be bought with care.

Items for resale

If you're looking for items you can resell at a profit, such as wholesale stock, then the net can be a beneficial tool for buying. The key here is to know your market – numerous non-eBay online auctions sell wholesale stock, be it cars, computers or other products, but if you are considering trying to buy any of these products and resell them for a profit, you should do your research before starting. Checking out issues like markets and prices will help you determine if suitable stock – at a good price – is available through the internet.

As for buying a single item and then selling it on for a quick profit, it's best to know your stuff. As we've discussed, it's possible to hunt out a misidentified item, which you can then buy on the cheap. You can subsequently turn a quick profit by relisting the item properly and selling it on at a far higher price. Being successful does require both luck and extensive knowledge of the particular market though – and probably wouldn't be enough of a regular revenue-generator to support you as your only source of income.

 Property

As it is the most expensive thing that many people will ever buy, property isn't something that comes to mind as ideal for purchasing on the internet. Actually, if you were to buy a property purely on the basis of a picture seen on a website, you'd be certifiable! However, the internet can be a very beneficial tool for finding potential purchases.

Many estate agents now have their own websites, where property details are uploaded at the same time they're put in the shop window. Additionally, many are members of larger sites that carry the listings of numerous estate agents. You can set search preferences and

have new listings matching your criteria e-mailed to you as soon as the properties are put up online.

This can be a great help in getting you 'early bird' information on suitable properties, and getting a jump on other potential buyers. There are also numerous sites with advice on finding property auctions, mortgages and more plus many mortgage brokers can also do you quotes online.

The internet is also an ideal place for those shopping for property abroad. Most holiday home vendors have extensive websites showing their stock and contacting them online will provide the easiest and cheapest way of getting in touch. Beware, though, of con-artists, as this is another area where scams are rife. If you are in the market for a Spanish villa, you'll want to check out what's available online, but do ensure whichever agent you're dealing with is legitimate. Ask for references, and check with previous clients.

Finally, there are properties advertised on eBay. Believe it or not, houses, flats, shops and even fields all get listed pretty regularly. This may seem mad, but in reality, is no less risky than buying at a real life auction where you won't be able to survey the property before buying. In fact, in many cases, it may be less risky as most owners will be (or should be) happy to let you look the property over before you bid, and you can always take a friendly surveyor or builder with you when you do so.

While the net is ideal for buying plane tickets, hotels and car rentals for your holiday, do try and book as far in advance as possible. There are countless websites dedicated to getting flights cheaply and as long as you're booking in advance, you can get some excellent rates. Many also act as one-stop shops that cover all aspects of your holiday, so you can sort everything out in one deal – and possibly get a discount in the process.

If you can't book far in advance, then it's a good idea to hold off buying for as long as possible. While flight prices usually increase the closer you get to the date of departure, they can drop in the last 24 hours as vendors rush to offload leftover seats. Air tickets can usually be booked direct through the carriers' websites too, so make sure you check them thoroughly as well – they may be even cheaper.

Most of these sites will also allow you to 'hold' bookings for a certain period of time. Often this is only for 24 or 48 hours, but if your booking is on 'hold' and the price subsequently increases, you'll still be able to buy your ticket within that window at the 'held' price.

Food

Many delivery-service restaurants offer online ordering which can be far easier than having to communicate your order to a phone operator. Some also do online specials that can save you a few pounds in cash, if not in weight!

Online grocery ordering from supermarkets is popular with busy people in metropolitan areas. Many supermarkets now offer online-ordering, where you submit a list of items you require, pay using a credit card, and then have them delivered to your home. Delivery is not free, and as items are pre-paid, if something is out of stock, be warned that a 'similar' item will be substituted. This will be selected by the shop itself, and in many cases, can be nothing like the original item requested.

Bargain point schemes

There are numerous schemes that send you sponsored links to competitions, surveys and the like, and in return for filling them out, you get points which can be added up and then discounted from purchases.

Unless you have endless free time on your hands (and get a kick out of seeing your inbox full of uninteresting spam and competition offers), we recommend you don't bother. It'll take you forever to accrue enough points to get anything out of having them, and by the time you've got to that point, the scheme may have gone out of business anyway.

SELLING

Now you have a good idea of what's involved in buying goods on the internet, you are probably wondering about the flip side of e-commerce. What about selling?

If you are interested in selling online, there are two main ways this can be done. Either selling at an online auction, or selling through your own website. Which one you choose will largely be dependent on how much you have to sell, and whether you want your selling to be a business or a hobby.

If getting rid of some clutter, or even wanting to thin out a collection by shedding duplicates, then listing your wares on an auction site is the way to go.

Running your own auction

Running your own eBay auctions is a quick and easy way to sell your wares. To begin with, register with the site as a seller – this requires filing credit card details with them, so seller's fees can be charged to this account. Bear in mind that if you registered as a buyer using an anonymous web-based e-mail address, such as Hotmail or Yahoo, then you'll need to register a credit card to get your user ID active for selling. This is so eBay can verify your details, as sellers are subject to stricter scrutiny than buyers.

The selling process

Once you're registered to sell, it is wise to invest in either a digital camera or a scanner as items without pictures are harder to sell, and it's free to include at least one image. Take clear photos, emphasising the elements of your item most likely to appeal to buyers. A digital camera is by far the quickest way to do this, but an acceptable alternative is to take pictures with a regular camera and get the images scanned. This is, however, rather more time-consuming and expensive.

When choosing a digital camera, don't be talked into buying one that does more than you need. There's no point buying a 5.0 mega-pixel beast of a camera, as for online auctions, a high resolution image simply isn't necessary, and eBay will automatically reduce the size of any huge images anyway.

You can pick up a perfectly acceptable digital camera for around

£70. It's what you show in the picture that matters, as better pictures attract more bids since people aren't put off by the fear that they won't be able to see any defects properly. If the item is flat, such as a book or CD, you can simply scan the item itself for maximum clarity.

So, you've got your item ready to sell, and a nice crisp image of it on your computer hard drive. What are the steps you need to take between here and making a sale on eBay?

Log in to eBay using the same username and password used for buying, and click on the 'Sell' link on eBay's main tool bar at the top of the page. This will take you on to the first stage of the selling process.

This first part will present you with two options, one for selling at online auction, the other for selling through a fixed price listing. A fixed price listing is where you set a price for the item, and the first person who bids that amount wins. There is no opportunity to bid less, and the price is stated on the item page – unlike a reserve price auction, where the reserve price is secret.

For now, keep things simple and choose to sell at auction. Fill the button for this choice, and then click on the 'Sell Your Item' button below.

While most people will search eBay by using the search function, it is also possible to browse items, and many collectors do just that; bookmarking the categories of interest to them, and monitoring them for any new items. First select your main

category and click continue. You can list an item in a second category as well, but this will double your listing fees and is not particularly recommended.

Clicking 'Continue' will take you through to a page with four windows. These contain the choices for subcategories. Let's say we are selling a 'Superman' comic. If you select 'Books, Comics & Magazines' as the main category, your first choice on this page will give you the main subcategories, which includes 'Comics'. Selecting this makes the next menu appear with even more refined subcategories. Here we should choose 'US Comics', and we will then be able to categorise our comic by date. Let's say our issue is from 1976, so we select the '1970 – 1979' option. The final menu allows you to choose the character name, so click on 'Superman'. A box beneath the menus will display a code number, this is the number of the category you have selected, and our item is now in exactly the right place for a US edition of a 1976 Superman comic.

The number of categories on eBay has grown at an alarming rate as the site has become more popular. If you are unsure of what category to place your item in, it's a good idea to do a quick search for similar items and see where they have been categorised.

Once you are satisfied that you have found the perfect place to sell your goods, click 'Continue' at the bottom of the screen. This will take you through to step two of the selling process: 'Describe Your Item'.

This is important and is where a little salesmanship can go a long way. Here you will give your auction a title and write the description that will hopefully entice browsers into placing a bid. When users enter keywords in the search engine, it is this title and text that they will be searching, so make sure you're as descriptive as possible – don't let the picture do all the talking! The more complete your description, the more confident potential bidders will feel.

Look at similar auctions to get ideas. You need the title to include as much information as possible, so state what the item is, ie. comic, vase or figurine. If it's a consumer product, say who made it, ie. Wedgwood, Sony, Gucci, etc. With our Superman comic, we'd want people to see it's a 1976 Superman Comic, and we should also give the volume, issue number and, if there's space, details of the condition. When writing the title, you need to think of all the words someone might be searching with if they were looking to find your item, and include as many as possible. You are limited to 55 characters in your title, however, so be as brief as possible. To maximise the use of this space use abbreviations where possible. Try to resist the urge to attract attention with multiple exclamation points or cries of "L@@K!!!" This looks cheap and silly, and will make you seem like a novice.

If you are not sure which keywords to include then, as always, try searching for similar items to get a feel for what works. Try different search terms and see how similar items come up with each keyword, and which ones get the highest number of bids and the highest sale prices.

Underneath the box for the title, there is the opportunity to include a subtitle. Use these sparingly – if at all – as it costs extra, and such text is not searchable. Depending on the category you're in, there may be additional choice boxes under this where you can select condition, year or other identifiers from drop-down menu boxes. It's a good idea to fill in as much of this information as possible, since it gives buyers good at-a-glance information about your item.

How much you write will depend on the item you are selling. If it is an electrical item, you should include all the features. If it is clothing, describe the style, colour, number of pockets and give measurements and size information. Always state the item's age and condition, making sure to mention any defects or marks, but basic sales techniques dictate that you should only do this after you have hammered home all the good points.

If you are selling an item in a collectors' market, such as the Superman comic example, then take the time to familiarise yourself with lingo that collectors' use. For instance, comics have a very specific grading system and while you might think your item is in very good condition, it may not correspond to the criteria for a comic that is officially in 'very good' condition. Don't list items as being in mint condition unless they are brand new; this is a common trick used by inexperienced sellers and will put off serious buyers who know there is no such thing as a second-hand item in perfect condition.

At this point, it is also a good idea to state what the charge will be for postage and packing, your returns policy and what action you will take if the item is not paid for. If buyers do not pay for items, they can be reported to eBay, who will investigate them. The seller can then claim back their final value fee from eBay and relist the item. If it sells the second time round, then the second listing fee will also be refunded. Though you will add this information again later, it never hurts to repeat it as prominently as possible.

Once you're happy with your description, click 'Continue' and move on to the third step: 'Pictures & Details.'

Choose the price at which you want the auction to start, the reserve price if you want to set one, and the buy-it-now option if you want to give your bidders the chance to buy the item immediately. When selecting a start price, it's important to think strategically. If your item is desirable and your listing written correctly, then you will get more bidders interested by starting at a very low start price. This builds excitement and gets interest, as bidders think they may get a bargain. They won't, but that perception will get your auction on plenty of 'watching' lists, and should guarantee a healthy final bid price. The other added benefit of a low start price is that you will pay less in fees. These increase incrementally depending on how high your start price is, as follows:

Start or Reserve	Insertion Fee
£0.01 - £0.99	£0.15
£1.00 - £4.99	£0.20
£5.00 - £14.99	£0.35
£15.00 - £29.99	£0.75
£30.00 - £99.99	£1.50
£100 - upwards	£2.00

March 2005

Next, select the duration of the auction, choosing from one, three, five, seven or ten day options. Most sellers prefer to list for ten days, as this gives the item exposure for the maximum length of time and allows bids to warm up to a nice fever pitch. If you're selling something where time is of the essence, like a concert ticket, you may want to put it on for a shorter period to highlight the urgency. You will find time sensitive and in-demand items such as this will sell quickly, so setting a high 'Buy It Now' price can yield dividends.

Once you've chosen the price, upload that all-important picture. eBay hosts one photograph for free, but charges for any additional pictures you put on their server, up to a total of five. Unless your item is expected to sell for a high price, or there is some benefit in showing it from different angles, there's no need to use anything other than your free image.

Uploading pictures to the eBay server is easy. Click the 'Browse' button by the window for the picture's location, and then use the pop-up window to find and select the picture on your hard drive. This is repeated for every additional picture you want to add. When you click 'Continue' at the end of the page, they will upload automatically.

If you have your own server, and the pictures are on there, you can use as many as you like for free. Simply click the tab for 'Your Own Web Hosting' instead of using the one for eBay's hosting and enter the web address of the picture you want to use. The system will link to it automatically. There are many free image hosting websites out there, such as PhotoBucket, and if you plan on using a lot of images in your auctions, signing up is a good idea.

This page also offers the option of adding additional features to your auction, like a gallery image, where a small picture of the item appears in the listings next to the item title, or 'Featured Gallery'

where your item appears at the top of a search, highlighted in bold. These are all extra-cost options and some can be quite expensive, so when deciding whether or not to use them, consider their cost relative to the item's actual value. Continuing from this page takes you through to step four of the process, 'Payment & Postage', but first the site will activate a small pop-up window as your pictures, if you've chosen to use eBay's hosting, are uploaded. This window will close as soon as the upload is complete.

The 'Payment & Postage' section is where all the details about postal charges and what payment methods you accept are listed. Although this information is already in the listing text, it is repeated here. The more places you feature this information the better, as you don't want the winning bidder quibbling over postage or sending a cheque when you specified PayPal.

Choose the methods of payment you are willing to accept carefully – PayPal is faster, but comes with charges. On the other hand, cheques need to be posted and can bounce.

Next choose where you will ship to – whether it's worldwide, to certain territories or only to your home country. Remember, if you don't ship worldwide, you may lose bids, as the item only appears in the countries where you will post to. Selling globally increases the market and can result in far higher-than-average prices.

Beneath this, specify exact postage cost by type (ie. £1.50 for First Class inland and £5.00 Flat Rate International) and your returns policy. All this is done with drop-down menus that are very simple to use. Finally, enter text for payment instructions. Here state time frames; how long after the auction you expect payment to be made, what course of action will be taken if payment is not forthcoming (for example, reporting to eBay and adding negative feedback) and any other terms and conditions you wish to place on the sale. Clicking 'Continue' at the bottom of this page takes you to the final step, 'Review & Submit'. Here, you can read through the auction in its entirety, checking spelling and details. Thankfully, there is an option to go back and edit any section.

At the bottom of this page, there is the final cost for starting the auction. Double check this (make sure you have not made a mistake with the start price) and then click the 'Submit Listing' button. Your auction will go onto eBay, and you have officially become an eBay seller!

All the auctions you're running will be listed in your 'My eBay' page so you can check on their progress. If anything goes wrong, such as if an item is lost or broken or you simply change your mind, you can end the auction at any point, whether there are bids or not, up until the last 24 hours. Once this deadline passes, you will no longer be able to stop it and will be obliged to sell to the highest bidder. This prevents sellers from pulling auctions at the very last minute if they are unhappy with the bids.

When the auction ends, you will automatically receive an e-mail informing you of the result. If there are no bids, you will get an e-mail offering the chance to relist the item. If the item has sold, there is a link to send an e-mail invoice to the winning bidder. As soon as payment has arrived or cleared, send the item by the agreed postal method. Prompt and courteous communication is the lifeblood of the eBay community, so don't sit around waiting for them to contact you – take the initiative and keep things moving. Once both parties are happy, positive feedback should always be left so other eBay users can see how reliable you are.

For every successful auction, you will have to pay a final value fee. Just as real life auction houses charge sellers a percentage of what their items sell for, eBay charges for items sold through their website.

You will be charged the listing fee plus the final value fee per auction. An invoice will be sent for your seller fees on a monthly basis. These will be charged to the credit card you placed on file when you registered. Payment can also be arranged by direct debit from a bank account, or be paid for by making a one-off PayPal payment. Leave fees unpaid for too long, and eBay will block you from starting any new auctions.

 Other details to remember

If you only have a few items to sell at online auction, the 'My eBay' page will be more than adequate for keeping track of your auctions. Once items have ended, they move to the 'Sold' section, where you can see at a glance if they have been paid for online, mark them paid if they've been paid by cheque, and flag them as posted when you've sent them out. You can also see whether or not you've received feedback on an item.

However, if you plan to use eBay to sell a high volume of product as a business, you'll want to invest in some of eBay's bulk-selling tools, like Sales Manager Pro, which replaces 'My eBay' for a subscription fee. This has far more features for the high-volume seller, enabling you to keep track of who's bought what, what has been paid for and which items are still to be mailed out, far more easily. If this sounds like you, then there are other tools worth investigating, such as Turbo-Lister, which allows bulk-uploading of auctions, as listing identical items one-by-one can be very time consuming.

You may even want to open an 'eBay shop' where items can be listed that are not included in the regular listings at cheaper insertion fees, or add an 'About Me' page where you describe yourself, your specialist selling area or your business. This option is available to casual users as well, and costs nothing.

In addition to the above, eBay does offer other seller incentives. From time to time, there will be a 'Free Listing Day' or a '5p Listing Day' when basic insertion fee costs will be lowered or dropped entirely for a day.

As well as making use of special promotions, the smart, cash-conscious eBay seller will also want to make sure their item is worth selling on eBay. Do this by searching the completed auctions (there is an option to do this on the 'Advanced Search' page) for similar items, and making sure they sold well enough to justify the time and trouble you will be taking to list your item. Many experienced sellers also choose to start ten day listings on a Thursday, so that their item will end the following Sunday. Many people choose to bid at the last second, so it's a good idea to time your auction to end when more of them will be at home to bid and not at work or asleep.

If you have an item which will appeal to bidders abroad, it is possible to list it directly on their local eBay site, although do take note that fee structures and other regulations may differ slightly from site to site. For example, on US eBay, a ten day auction costs extra to set up, while only the UK version of eBay requires that reserve prices be £50 or more. If you're selling overseas, then also take into account time differences between countries. There's not much benefit in setting your American auction to end at a reasonable hour in the UK, but five o'clock in the morning in the US!

Finally, remember that the examples of insertion and final value fees given here are only the basic fees for eBay UK. Optional auction extras, such as gallery insertion or bold headlines, will add to these costs. In addition, fees for items like cars and property will differ.

You will also want to review all of eBay's rules to make sure your items are not going to fall foul of the law. If you contravene the rules, the listing may be pulled from eBay and if you offend repeat-edly, then you may find yourself banned from trading. Some items cannot be listed on eBay at all, and the following is a basic list of forbidden items:

Airline Tickets
Alcohol
Animal/Wildlife Products

Catalogue/URL Sales –

(ie. sales linking to an external website)

Fake currency or stamps

Fake trademarked items – (i.e. fake designer clothes)

Credit cards

Drugs, and all related items

Embargoed goods

Guns & Ammunition

Fireworks

Franking Machines

Football tickets

Government IDs, licences or uniforms

Human body parts & remains

Items that have been subject to product recall

Lock-picking devices

Lottery tickets

Mailing lists/personal information

Offensive material

Prescription drugs

Pyramid financial gain schemes

Shares & securities

Stolen property

Surveillance equipment

Tobacco products

Train tickets

Travel vouchers

Unlocking software

Check out the eBay help pages to check if your item can be safely sold on eBay. Even though it sounds like common sense, you should review their many rules for seller behaviour, which include not bidding on your own items, not offering to sell outside of eBay and not trying to extort anything from other users by threatening negative feedback.

Finally, if you feel you've got plenty of items that could sell on eBay, but just don't have the time or inclination to do so yourself, then you can always look for an eBay 'Drop Shop'.

These are companies not affiliated with eBay that will list your items for you in return for a cut of the proceeds. The advantages of services like this are that they employ expert listings writers who will make sure items are listed properly, have excellent photographing capabilities and have their own servers, so can upload as many pictures of an item as they like. They will also take care of payments, packing and posting items and as such take a lot of the hassle out of selling on eBay for the casual seller.

Most 'Drop Shops' will take around one third of the item's final price in return for their services, but as their high-quality descriptions should ensure the item gets a higher price, this will most likely offset the cost. Most, however, will only take higher-value items. It is not worth their time and money to pay their listers, photographers and packers to manage auctions for items, which will only sell for small amounts and therefore will not earn them decent commissions.

Your own website

The second major way to sell online is by setting up your own, dedicated website. This is the option that makes the most sense if you're running a business, rather than just an individual clearing out some junk.

As mentioned before, selling online has great advantages for the retailer – and in this case, that's you. If you have a retail business that you want to take online, it may be as an alternative to selling through a shop or you may choose to run the website alongside a bricks-and-mortar store. Either way, the website will have the following advantages.

1. It will save you cash
You won't need to pay shop staff rent on premises or power bills.

Running a website will take far less manpower than a shop as orders can go directly to your database – if it's set up properly.

2. You'll reach a wider market

With an online shop, you won't just be limited to the people who walk past your window; you reach potential buyers from all over the world. This also eliminates the need to find a suitable location for your business. What's more suitable than a shop which doesn't require rent and has the potential to reach millions of buyers every day?

3. You can improve customer service

Lower overheads mean lower prices and all customer questions, complaints or feedback can come via e-mail so can be dealt with quickly and easily. All of this means you'll be able to build a bigger, better customer base that will keep coming back for more – as long as your service remains at a high level.

4. You can be open 24-7

A website is open all the time, allowing customers to shop whenever they feel like it, hence increasing the volume of business.

5. You can track stock more easily

With orders coming in directly to your database, you'll be able to see immediately what sells and what doesn't. This will enable you to eliminate lines that aren't selling and stock up on lines that are.

6. You'll have an online catalogue for customers

If you still retain a real world shop, customers thinking of visiting can look and see what you sell online.

Setting up your own selling website isn't a decision to be taken lightly. While it will cost far less than opening up a real world shop, there are numerous considerations to mull over before you get started.

First of all, consider what you want the website to do for you. Will it primarily be for selling or for displaying your products? How will it focus on target markets? You need to put together an outline of the site's content, deciding what the most important information is that you want to include: product information, contact details, locations, etc. Think about how the design of the website will appeal to your target market.

Will you want to create the website yourself? If you have moderate IT skills, and the site you want to put together isn't too complicated, you may well be able to do this. Alternatively, you can hire a professional designer to build a site to your specifications, although this will add to the costs, and you'll be reliant on them for future changes and updates.

You then need to arrange hosting for the site on a server – the place where the pages are stored so that net users can access them. Paying for this hosting can end up being your biggest ongoing cost, so shop around. Don't automatically opt for the one with the lowest monthly charge. You'll want a host that won't sting you with higher charges when all that lucrative web traffic starts rolling in.

Think about your URL – the web address that you'll use for the site. It should be something that's immediately identifiable with

your business. Check that it is not already taken, or buy it back if it has already been registered and the current owner is willing to sell it. Once you have found one you like, for a very small fee, register it in your name.

 DIY or professional?

It's going to be far cheaper if you build the site yourself. Although more costly, a good web designer will bring added advantages. For example, they will be skilled at making sure the website fits your image, and the image which will best attract potential clients. They will also know how to structure websites so information is easily accessible.

A professional designer is also more likely to be familiar with the sort of modern web technology you may well want to use, such as encrypting web pages and integrating search engines. This is all necessary stuff if you are going to want to sell through the site at any sort of volume. Of course, it is entirely possible to take the DIY route. For a very basic site, there are ready-made internet pages where you just add pictures and words to create your own instant website. These are often offered by internet service providers, web-hosting companies and software manufacturers but their generic style won't do you any favours if you want to impress customers.

Alternatively, you can opt for a software package to give you a little more creative freedom. Most major software manufacturers now offer web-editing software which allows you to design pages more or less from scratch, thus avoiding the cheap, formatted look a site can get if you go with templates. These programs can simplify the nuts and bolts of making a website, however you'll still need a basic understanding of web technology and some design skills. If you don't have these, then acquiring them can take some time.

In the end, it comes down to a question of cost. If you can afford to go for a designer, the benefits speak for themselves. However, in picking a designer, try to use someone who is recommended. Check that they have designed and built similar websites, and that these have been successful. Ask them to refer you to sites they have designed and make sure they're easy to navigate and look good. See if they have any ideas of their own for your site and, if so, whether these fit in with what you have in mind.

Ensure that the designer will actually build the site for you, and not just design it. Check also if they can help with hosting and what support they offer to maintain the site after it goes live. You may need to learn how to do this yourself, or hire another web developer to do it. It is important to check copyright issues; make sure they assign ownership of the site, the design and the address over to you. Before any work commences, make sure you know upfront how the costs will be calculated. Will they charge an hourly rate, or a flat fee for the project?

Hosting

If anyone is to actually find and use your website, you'll have to get it hosted on a server. Servers are, quite simply, places where web pages are stored so the public can access them.

Hosting packages will probably be available from your existing internet service provider, so see what deals they can offer. If you want more flexibility, then look into using a dedicated web hosting company – find a balance between an acceptable monthly cost and a reasonable bandwidth allocation. Bandwidth is what your visitors will use every time they visit your page and going over your limit can incur nasty fees, or worse, your site going offline.

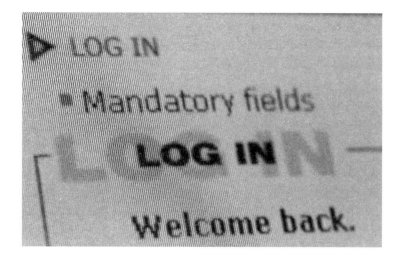

You can also purchase and set up your own web server to host your site on, though this is both expensive and technically complex. This may be the best option if your business can support it, but for a small shopping site, it's probably the equivalent of using the proverbial sledgehammer to crack a nut.

 Domain names

Branding is important so try and get your business name to be your website address i.e. www.yourcompanynamehere.co.uk. This will make it easy for potential customers to find you online. It can also be a good idea to register variations on your name, and the names of your primary products and services, and have these addresses redirect visitors automatically to your main site.

Registering a web address costs around £20 to £30 per name for a year but before you can register an address, you need to check whether or not it's available. For addresses ending with the .co.uk suffix, you can visit the Nominet website (an organisation which deals with UK internet addresses). For addresses with any other suffix, try InterNIC.

If the name isn't available, but the current owner is willing to sell it, buy it from them – although be warned that popular domain names can be expensive. Where possible, try abbreviations or variations on your company name. Otherwise, you may be able to register the name with your service provider or hosting company. Some hosts will offer free URL names – although these will generally include their own name (something like www.nameofhostingcompanyhere.yourcompanynamehere.co.uk). This may not send out the right message about your business, so do tread warily, as the savings you make in registration costs may well be negated by the business you'll lose for not looking professional.

Promoting your site

Ensure your web address is prominently displayed in any advertising, as well as on business cards, shop fronts and vehicles. Many of your customers will come directly to the site by typing this in their browser.

However, many more will find you – on purpose or by accident – by using a search engine. To ensure that this happens, make a list of all the most popular search engines – Google, Yahoo, Altavista – and register your site with these. You can usually do this by going to the homepage of the search engine you want to register with and looking for a button or link something along the lines of 'Submit Your URL Here'. Add your site to their database. If you can't see this option, then go to the site's 'Help' section and search for submission instructions from there.

Actually getting your site into search engines can take a while – some make you wait after registering, while they consider whether or not to include you; they also may want payment in return for inclusion.

On a search engine, however, you will be competing for position with an awful lot of similar websites. In order to make sure you come up close to the top, ensure that there are plenty of keywords contained in your pages pertaining to the product you're selling or the service you're offering. This will make sure that the pages crop up in searches as often as possible. Websites also have something called metatags, a list of invisible words that are only picked up by search engines. Use these to make sure you don't miss any relevant searches.

Many search engines also rank sites according to how many other websites have links to them. Try and ensure that as many as possible link to your site. You can participate in a link exchange programme, whereby you put links to other sites on yours, and they link to you in return, in order to boost everyone's ratings with the search engines. You should also resubmit your details to all the major services on a regular basis to stay near the top of their search lists.

Besides using search engines, there are various other methods to boost traffic to your site. Advertising, both online and in print, can offer more immediate and focused results than the somewhat scattershot search engines. Use ads on sites which will be of interest to the sort of people you are marketing your products to, as many will click through from banners and links on these sites if they see something that catches their eye.

You can, of course, send out mailings or e-mailings promoting your site. It is illegal to send unsolicited e-mail, or spam, so avoid the temptation to bombard every address you find with news of your site. Spamming people isn't the best way to build a solid customer base either!

Make sure you are listed in any directories, online or print, which list similar businesses or services. In addition, make sure there's a 'Tell A Friend' automatic e-mail button on your homepage so surfers can send details of your shop to their mates – all of whom are potential customers!

 Online shopping specifics

All the above advice can apply to any website created to promote a business, whether you actually want to sell through it, or just to use it as a showcase. However, there are other things you will need to take into consideration if you intend to sell through your site.

Do make sure you have the capacity to deliver your products speedily, efficiently and cost-effectively. As an internet consumer, you will already know to watch out for excessive delivery charges, so make sure that as a retailer you don't add these to your prices and lose customers in the process. Estimate how much volume you'll be shipping per month, and then get quotes and 'regular customer' discount rates for bulk shipping from

courier companies. You'll want to ensure that the delivery options you have are fast as well; nobody wants to wait for ages to get their order, especially in a world where 24 hour turnaround is fast becoming the norm. Swift customer service will make sure that clients come back again and again. Ideally, you should be able to quote several shipping options with different prices depending on how fast the items will arrive. Don't forget that you will also need packaging materials, so budget for these too. Boxes, tape, bubble-wrap and envelopes all eat into your profits if you let them.

Secondly, you'll need to have clear information as to how customers can contact you. Give your business name, address, telephone and fax numbers, e-mail address, as well as information on opening hours. Websites may be there 24 hours a day, seven days a week, but staff won't be and people like to have a human point of contact.

Lastly, and most importantly, work out how you will accept payment and ensure that this is displayed prominently on your site. While most online customers want to pay by credit or debit card, there are still plenty of people who won't give out card details over the internet so offer an alternative method. There are three ways of accepting credit and debit cards, and arrangements will need to be made for at least one of these before you start taking card payments. Option one is to set up a merchant account with a bank, option two is to use a payment-processing company; and option three is to set up your internet shop inside a virtual shopping mall.

 ## Merchant accounts

These are offered by nine different UK banks, and it's highly likely that if you have a business account, it will be with one of them. They are:

Alliance and Leicester

American Express

Bank of Scotland

Barclaycard Merchant Services

Diners Club

HSBC

Lloyds TSB Cardnet

NatWest/Royal Bank of Scotland Streamline

Ulster Bank

These banks are called merchant acquirers or acquiring banks. You may well already have a merchant account to accept payments for transactions if you have a regular shop, but you will also need a separate one for online payments. They work by allowing card-holders to make payment directly into the merchant account, with funds becoming available three-to-four working days later. One thing to watch out for here is fraud. Since online card payments are classed as what's called 'cardholder not present' transactions, if a transaction turns out to be fraudulent, the money can be reclaimed from your merchant account. This can happen even if the payment is authorised by the cardholder's bank. If the holder then claims the transaction is fraud, they can usually get their money back. You will need to have your site on a secure server in order to protect your customers' card details, too, since they will be submitting these directly to you.

Setting up a merchant account for your online payments may not be the best way to go if you don't sell in enormous volume, as there are regular costs involved. You may have to pay a sign-up fee of £200 or so, and there may be a fixed fee for receiving payments thereafter, or the bank may take a percentage of each sale; credit card payments may have a commission fee levied on them, while debit cards usually have fixed fees.

Also, many small businesses may not meet the requirements to open such an account. Banks that offer merchant accounts for card payments will want to see;

- A business plan, including cashflow details and promotional activities for your online services
- Your web address
- Full details of your products and services
- Full details of your suppliers
- Details of the delivery methods you'll be using and your terms and conditions
- Details of the secure server your transactions will be carried out on
- The anticipated average online transaction value and the estimated turnover your online selling is expected to generate

- Audited business bank accounts
- Bank and credit history details
- Trading history details
- Full contact details of all directors and partners in the business

As such, it may not be worth your while opening such an account if you are just starting out in online retail. In this case, you may want to consider the alternative ways of handling online payments.

 Payment processing companies

These are companies which take the payment from the customer's card, then send the money on to you. As such, they are a very manageable alternative for businesses with smaller turnover or those that don't meet the criteria for opening a merchant account.

The advantages of payment processing companies include the hassle they save you by removing the need to keep card details or handle the administration required by a merchant account. In addition, the application procedures for getting a payment processing account is generally less stringent than that for a merchant account.

There are, however, some drawbacks; customers will be able to see that their payment isn't going straight to you, and this may worry some of them and cause them not to buy. Also, some of these companies will not release funds until long after they have come in, sometimes up to four weeks later, and this may well impede cash flow within your operation.

Needless to say, these companies also charge for their services. Some may even have higher fees than merchant accounts, although if you shop around you should be able to find good deals,

since this is a highly competitive market. Many also offer insurance policies to protect you against fraud as, once again, if a card is used fraudulently, the amount charged on it can be claimed back from your business.

 Online shopping malls

If you're looking at using online selling in addition to a regular real world shop, then using an internet shopping mall can be a good idea.

We covered online shopping malls earlier – they are websites where numerous different shopping outlets can be found. For the seller, this means that the mall can host your shop and take any payments made on your behalf.

Using a mall can be beneficial to a small business. Many specialise in targeting a certain demographic of customer; others specialise in marketing certain types of product. Some will also give you software to get your shop started, which can be great if you don't want to hire a web designer, or if you want to design your own shop, but aren't sure where to start.

After your shop is open, it's up to you to maintain it, post updates and keep your stock, but the mall will take care of the vast majority of admin work for you. They also give help and technical support, and have the added bonus of being able to get you up and running almost instantly – the application process is a lot less laborious than with merchant accounts or payment companies.

Some malls are now going even further in what they offer. If, for example, you are a designer that wants your artwork or designs on mugs or t-shirts, you can sign up with a mall selling just these products, and you won't even need to provide your own stock. Just advertise your designs in your shop and when an order is placed, the mall will take care of the printing and despatching of the item to the buyer.

Malls are provided by many internet service providers as well as numerous companies that specialise in online sales venues. For sellers specialising in a specific area, malls can help target your product, and your relevant trading association may be able to put you in touch with a suitable one to get started.

However, there are drawbacks. They are an expensive way to establish an online selling site; with a joining fee and a percent-age of each sale going to the mall operator, and often work out more expensive than the cost of processing your own payments. In addition, there may be a monthly or yearly rental fee. Finally,

while the start-up software can be a boon to the less web-literate, you will likely find it ties you in to the mall's corporate identity and standard format, which may leave you struggling to stamp your identity on your own shop.

Secure areas

Whatever method of accepting online payments you eventually do choose, you need to ensure that any part of the website where sensitive information is entered such as names, credit card details, addresses, phone numbers or e-mails, is secure.

Putting these measures into place with encryption and secure servers can be complex and expensive, and are best left to a professional, unless you have advanced IT skills. Customers won't order if they don't think their information is secure.

Other requirements

If you do decide to sell online, there are a few other requirements that your site must meet:

1. You will need to provide the full name and contact details of your business, including an e-mail address. Over and above the fact that your customers will need to contact you to buy stuff, you are legally required to do this.

2. If applicable, you must display your VAT number.

3. Prices must be indicated clearly. If you decide not to include VAT in the prices as displayed (not a good idea, as it annoys potential buyers greatly), then this must be stated somewhere on the bill. You must also clearly state all delivery costs before a transaction is completed.

4. Give details of any and all trade associations, professional bodies or other similar schemes that your business belongs to. Not only will this reassure buyers that you are legitimate, it also gives them recourse to complain to someone in the unlikely event that a sale goes wrong.

5. Give a clear outline of your order process. Make it clear throughout the ordering process what stage the customer is at, and ensure that they know what information they will need to enter to complete their order.

6. Send electronic receipts immediately. Your system must be set up to automatically acknowledge that an order has been taken, even if your card processing system has not yet taken payment.

7. Give customers the opportunity to check their order. Before submitting to the sale, they should be able to read it through in its entirety and correct any mistakes before submitting payment.

8. Display your terms and conditions. These should be prominently displayed, and the customer should be able to save or print them easily.

9. Tell buyers how they can find information on any online conduct codes relevant to their order.

10. Ensure subsequent marketing e-mails are identified as such. These must be easily identified as communications that are commercial in nature, and must make it equally clear who has sent them. You are allowed to send marketing e-mails to existing customers, provided they have actively agreed to receive them. A tick box at the end of the order should be included for this purpose.

11. Unsolicited e-mail must be identifiable as such. It is still legal to send unsolicited mail to business accounts, but it is against the law to spam personal e-mail addresses. Since 2003, you can be fined up to £5,000 for each spam e-mail you send.

12. Give full details of discounts or sales. If you are offering any promotions or money-off specials, then make sure all terms and conditions are clear.

Finally, as an online seller you must also comply fully with the rules on distance selling (available from www.dti.gov.uk) and as you will be electronically storing customer data, you will also need to make sure your storage systems comply with the Data Protection Act. Information on this can be found at www.informationcommissioner.gov.uk.

 ## Common mistakes

There are numerous mistakes made by online sellers which are guaranteed to annoy potential customers and lose you business. Make sure your website doesn't fail you by getting caught in any of the following traps:

Wrong or outdated information
Nothing is more annoying than putting through an order only to be told the product is out-of-stock, discontinued or otherwise unavailable. Make sure your website is updated regularly.

Complicated site design or ordering process
You want customers to be able to find all the products you have available as easily as possible, so they can buy them on impulse without any extra effort. Remember, they're shopping from the

comfort of their home, so they've got nothing to lose if they leave your website empty-handed. The online shopper only has to decide that your site is not worth the bother because they can't find the information they want, and you've lost a sale. This is one major reason to bring in a professional web designer who knows how to construct a site for intuitive use. Saving money up front on a DIY site won't be a saving at all if you can't generate sales.

Bad customer service/late delivery

People expect service for their money. If they have to e-mail or call chasing their order, they will very likely take their order elsewhere next time. Make sure items are shipped on time and that calls and e-mails are answered promptly and courteously. If there are problems with an order, let the buyer know. They are much less likely to get annoyed if they know what's going on. Also, you may want to consider offering online tracking of purchases. This way, customers can see if their package has been dispatched. This will also cut down on the time you spend answering order enquiries.

Missing contact information

Buyers get jumpy if they think they won't be able to contact you, and rightfully so. If your contact information is buried in your site then it may look as if you've got something to hide, and shoppers will very likely surf elsewhere to spend their money.

Lack of description/pictures

Make sure that there are plenty of images of your products and ensure that these are as clear as possible. Ensure that well-written descriptions are included. Both text and pictures should combine to show your product off at its absolute best, so turn to professionals if you are unsure about doing it yourself.

Money-back guarantee

If you offer a money-back guarantee advertise it prominently, this will make shoppers feel far more at ease – it is far easier to part with money for something if you know you can get the money back should the item not live up to expectations.

Offer human customer support

This is especially important if your items are expensive. Buyers are far more likely to buy if they can talk to someone about their purchase on the phone before they commit to payment.

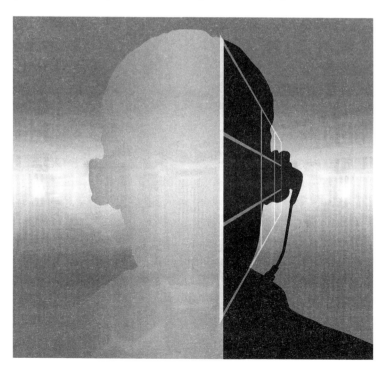

Online classifieds

The final way to sell online is through classified ads. There are many sites where you can post these, and these are at least as good as similar advertising in real life. Indeed, they are often better, given the ease with which consumers can browse ads online without having to buy a paper or magazine.

If you decide to place one of these, make sure you target it properly; for example, advertise a classic car up for sale on an owners' club or enthusiast website if possible. This way, you will target the people most likely to be interested in what you have for sale.

Online ads also allow you more anonymity, as you can just give an e-mail address instead of a phone number. One word of caution, though. Never give out your own personal e-mail address for these ads, as you risk being picked up by spam merchants. Instead, create a disposable Hotmail, Yahoo or Gmail account to use for the purpose of the ad.

WHAT IF IT ALL GOES WRONG?

You've now read this book. Maybe you've taken the plunge and bought online. But what if something does go wrong, despite you being cautious? The key is not to panic.

Know your rights

The action you can take in the case of a internet purchase going wrong can vary, depending on the product and the nature of the problem. Rest assured that you will almost always be able to do something about it and will often be able to recover your money in full.

Whatever the individual retailer's policies are, they must still operate within the guidelines set out by the law. British law states that any goods sold over the internet have to be of a satisfactory quality and must be fit to carry out the purpose they were intended for. In other words, clothes can't fall apart after a few washes, fridges must keep things cold and microwaves must heat food properly.

If the item does not perform as it should then you are legally entitled to get your money back, although you should act quickly, in order to prove you made your claim within a reasonable amount of time, and that you did not wilfully do any of the damage yourself. If you paid by credit card, you may be able to claim your money back from the card company, as well as pursuing the vendor for a refund. In addition, credit cards should also cover you for consequential loss, where a fault with your purchase causes damage to other items. For example, if your new washing machine starts leaking and floods the house, destroying your carpets, you will be able to claim back not only the cost of the washing machine, but also the cost of the carpets. Check with your credit card company to find out what their policy is, but most will cover you provided the damage costs over £275 to put right.

Laws on distance selling

In 2000, the EU brought into force new laws regarding distance selling. Distance selling is defined as any method of trading where vendor and customer are not present in each other's company for a transaction – specifically this covers catalogue sales by mail-order, telesales and buying over the internet.

In England, these laws form part of the Consumer Protection (Distance Selling) Regulations 2000. Your rights under these regulations include the following:

1. You have the right to be given clear and specific information about any goods or services offered before you decide to make a

purchase. Descriptions must be explicit, and any deviation from this (unless it is specified that products may differ from descriptions) is unacceptable.

2. You have the right to receive confirmation of these descriptions when you buy a product or service. When you make a purchase, you must be told in writing exactly what it is you have purchased. Any deviation between the item you receive and the confirmation is against the law.

3. You must be given a week-long 'Cooling Off' period.
Retailers are obliged to give you seven days to change your mind about the purchase and to back out of the contract, as long as the merchandise is returned in the condition it was sent out. Take note that certain items aren't covered by this regulation. These include DVDs, CDs and video tapes which have been used and also food, flowers and other fresh produce which can spoil.

4. Credit card issuers must protect you against credit card fraud. If your card details are stolen and used without your consent by another individual online, then your card issuer must refund you the costs accrued by the fraudster.

Buying internationally – outside the EU

If the site you've bought from is outside of the European Union, any potential issues can be rather more difficult to resolve, as they may not be subject to the EU laws, and you can have little or no protection. It is wise to exercise great caution when buying from international territories.

When it comes to credit card protection for purchases made outside the EU, different card issuers may have different rules, but it is entirely possible that they are in no way liable for problems with international purchases. While most will entertain claims for the value of a faulty item if it was bought outside the EU, they will generally not be willing to cover any consequential loss caused by the item.

How to complain

If the goods reach your doorstep and you are not happy with them, either because they're broken or they just don't match their description, always start by contacting the seller.

When you made your purchase, you should have bookmarked or printed out the customer service contact details. If they list a phone number then call and explain the problem. E-mail may seem more convenient, but is easily lost or ignored. Give the operator as much information as you can, including your order number, how you paid, how much and when. Always ask for the name of the person you speak to, and ask for a case number which you can write down and quote if you have contact them again.

Explain why you are dissatisfied with your purchase and clearly state whether you want a refund or a replacement item. If you aren't satisfied with the initial response you get, move up the chain of command, complaining in writing to the company's head office if need be. Remember that if the goods are faulty or not as advertised, you are legally entitled to a refund or a replacement. This goes for services bought, as well as physical items.

If your claim is not settled, then be sure to keep copies of any and all correspondence via e-mail or post, and take note of

what was said in phone conversations. You can even record conversations if you have a suitable recorder, but should your claim come to court, you are legally required to inform the other party that they are being recorded before you start the conversation for it to be admissible as evidence. This is why

whenever you call a customer helpline, you are often informed in advance that calls may be recorded or monitored for training purposes.

If the person is informed that they have been recorded after the recording has been made, or if you don't inform them at all, not only will the tapes be inadmissible but the other party on the phone can sue you.

What if the seller won't play ball?

If you do not get satisfaction through a direct complaint to the seller, check their site for the TrustUK logo, or evidence of any other professional body. If they are a member of a trade body then file a complaint with them. You should also contact your local Trading Standards Department, which you can find by going to www.tradingstandards.gov.uk.

 What if my product never shows up?

If you believe the product was advertised in a misleading manner on a website then contact the Advertising Standards Authority (ASA). Internet advertising must be compliant with the British Codes of Advertising and Sales Promotion. This states that all adverts must adhere to the law, not be indecent and must also be honest and truthful in the claims they make about items and their descriptions of them. Take note, however, that this only applies to British websites, and won't cover claims made by manufacturers on their own websites.

The law requires that any item or service ordered must be delivered or rendered within 30 days of the order being placed. If this is not the case then, unless you have agreed to a longer waiting period in advance, you will be able to claim your money back from the company just as if the goods were faulty.

Financial products are one of the areas where you should be particularly careful when purchasing, as any problems are likely to end up costing you more than the initial price. While you will be protected under the same consumer laws that govern buying anything else on the internet, getting your money back if you've invested it with a company of dubious repute can take a very long time. However, there are a couple of simple precautions you can take.

All businesses which offer financial products must have authorisation to do so from the Financial Services Authority (FSA). The FSA regulates most financial services within the UK, so before parting with any money to an internet finance company of any sort, it's a good idea to check that they are authorised to offer the service you're buying – don't just take the company's word for it. Similarly, if the company you are dealing with is based elsewhere in the EU, you can check that the company is legally allowed to offer financial services by contacting the Public Enquiries Office.

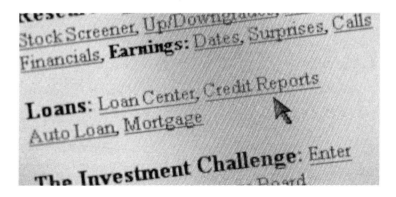

A–Z INTERNET SHOPPING JARGON BUSTER

Grasping the basics of buying and selling on the internet is one thing. Understanding what all the jargon means is quite another! The following are some of the most common words, phrases and names used in this book.

Account

If you put your details into any website and can access the site again by signing in with your username and password, then you have created an account at that site.

Add-on costs

The additional costs charged in order to cover the cost of postage and packing.

Advertising Standards Authority

The regulatory body which ensures that all adverts in the UK, online or otherwise, adhere to guidelines of good taste and don't break the law in terms of the claims they make.

Auction
A sale where people place bids for how much they are willing to pay for the item. The highest bidder buys the item for the amount they bid.

Bid Increment
The amount by which an interested party must increase their offer in order to become the highest bidder.

Bidding
The act of making an offer for an auction item.

Browser
A computer program used to access the internet.

Buy-It-Now
A selling format on eBay, whereby the seller states a price at which buyers can purchase the item immediately, without having to bid. A bidder agreeing to pay this price ends the auction immediately.

Checkbox

A small, empty 'box' on a web page. When clicked, a tick will appear in it, marking your agreement to the statement or option.

Comparison Shopping Agent

An online search engine which searches for the price of similar items on many different websites allowing you to compare deals.

Consequential Loss

Damage caused by a faulty item to something other than the item itself.

Cookie

A small computer file downloaded onto a computer's hard drive to retain site preferences, passwords and usernames.

Customs & Excise Department

The government department in charge of levying taxes and duties on items for sale.

Disposable E Mail Account

A free online e-mail account which can be opened with little fuss, allowing it to be easily abandoned when no longer required.

Distance Selling

A sale where customer and vendor do not meet. These can be carried out online, over the telephone or by mail order.

Domain Name

The online address at which you will find a particular website, in the format http://www.domain-name.com. See also web address, URL.

Download
To 'download' is to request information, a program or anything else off of the internet and move it from the internet to your computer hard drive.

Drop Shop
A business which will auction items online on your behalf in return for a percentage of the proceeds.

Encryption Software
A method of transmitting sensitive data so it cannot be accessed while in transit.

Feedback
A voluntary comment left for a buyer or seller on eBay, based on how well a transaction went.

Final Value Fees
A component of the fee charged to a seller by eBay for a successful auction, calculated on the final price at which the item sold.

Financial Services Authority
The regulatory body governing all companies offering financial services in the UK.

Fixed Price Listing

A selling format on eBay, whereby a seller offers an item at one fixed price to buyers, with no option of bidding any less or more.

Freeware

Software that is available from its manufacturer for free.

Frequently Asked Questions (FAQ)

The section of a website where you can find answers to commonly asked questions about the site and its services.

Grey Import

A vehicle imported to the UK for the express purpose of resale, usually from Japan.

Holding Booking

Placing a 'hold' on a ticket booking, in order to keep it saved for you at that price for a fixed period of time, regardless of whether or not the price increases during this period.

Hosting

A computer hard drive which stores web pages and allows these to be accessed by other computers is said to be 'hosting' the pages.

Insertion Fees

A component of the fees charged to sellers by eBay, calculated on the start price of an auction as listed.

Merchant Bank Account

A bank account which can accept credit card payments directly.

Online mall

A website made up of numerous online shops, usually with some sort of common theme.

Online Payment System

A website which can accept payment for an auction or other service via the internet.

Online receipt

A receipt issued by a seller for a transaction, appearing either as a web page immediately after the transaction has been processed, or in an e-mail sent to the buyer afterwards.

Partner Sites

A site which pays another site to link to it, or to advertise its products in searches.

Payment Processing Company

A company which accepts credit card payments on behalf of another business.

Pop-Up

A new browser window which 'pops up' when a link is clicked.

Privacy Policy

A website's policy regarding the selling or sharing of information gathered about its customers.

Public Enquiries Office

The regulatory body governing, among other things, the legality of EU companies trading in financial products in the UK.

Radio Button

A small empty circle which can be filled with a dot when clicked in order to make a selection.

Reserve Price

An eBay feature, whereby a seller sets a price higher than the start price, but which is the lowest price at which they are prepared to sell, regardless of whether or not there are lower bids.

Run-Out

An item which has been discontinued and is now being sold off cheap to make way for a newer model.

Sales Tax

An American tax added to any purchase for domestic US consumption. This is added at the till in US stores, and is not included in the price as displayed. It should not be charged on products being bought for export.

Secure Area

The section of a website protected by encryption software to keep sensitive data safe from hackers.

Secure Connection

A connection to a website that falls under the protection of encryption software, shown by a closed padlock in the corner of your browser.

Seller Fees

Charges set by eBay and other online auction sites, following a successful auction, based on the final selling price.

Selling tools

Programmes and features provided by eBay, sometimes at a cost, to help sellers track their auctions more easily.

Shipping Costs

The amount added by any seller to an item to cover the cost of sending it to the buyer.

Shopping Basket/Cart

A feature of many online shops where you virtually store the items you want to purchase, while browsing the site for further items to buy.

Sniping

Bidding on an auction at the very last second in order to avoid being outbid.

Spam

The e-mail equivalent of junk mail.

Spyware

Programs which download to a computer's hard drive either through surfing or packaged within a downloaded program. These then spy on the computer's user, transmitting details about their internet surfing habits back to a third party.

SSL (Secure Sockets Layering)

A common encryption system, used to protect data from hackers while it is in transit over the internet.

Starting Price

The price at which a seller starts the bidding when listing an auction.

Trading Standards Department

The organisation in charge of regulating all sellers in the UK.

Upload

To send any information from your computer to the internet.

Username

The name chosen by a user to be the ID for use in a website account.

URL

Uniform Resource Locator. See Domain Name.

VAT (Value Added Tax)

A 17.5% tax added to certain items sold in the UK.

Watching

Monitoring an eBay auction without placing a bid by adding it to the 'My eBay Page'.

Web Address

See Domain Name and URL.

Web Page

A single screen on a website, containing information and links to other pages.

Website

A series of interlinked web pages.

Wish List

A list held at an online shopping site such as Amazon, where you can store details of items you would like to purchase at some point, but without committing to a purchase.

USEFUL WEBSITE ADDRESSES

Auctions

www.auctioning4U.co.uk

www.eBaymotors.com

www.eBay.co.uk

www.eBid.co.uk

Banking

www.alliance-leicester.co.uk

www.barclays.co.uk

www.egg.co.uk

www.lloydstsb.com

www.rbs.co.uk

www.americanexpress.co.uk

www.dinersclub.com

www.hsbc.co.uk

www.natwest.com

www.ulsterbank.com

Classified ads

www.autotrader.co.uk

www.exchangeandmart.co.uk

www.loot.co.uk

Discount outlet directories

www.designer.co.uk

www.topoftheshops.co.uk/Clothing_and_designers

Domain registration

www.interNIC.co.uk

www.nominet.org.uk

Entertainment

www.dvdtohome.co.uk

www.myvue.com

www.screenselect.co.uk

www.ugccinemas.co.uk

www.lovefilm.com

www.odeon.co.uk

www.ticketmaster.co.uk

Food

www.ocado.co.uk

www.pizzahut.co.uk

www.tesco.com

Information & the law

www.asa.org.uk

www.dti.gov.uk

www.dvla.gov.uk

www.fsa.gov.uk

www.hmce.gov.uk

www.tradingstandards.gov.uk

Online shopping malls

www.cafeshops.com

www.shopatworldpay.com

http://shopping.yahoo.co.uk

www.worldwideshoppingmall.co.uk

www.ishop.co.uk

www.shopping.co.uk

www.TheVirtualMall.co.uk

Online payment services

www.bidpay.com

www.nochex.com

www.paypal.co.uk

Price comparison sites

www.comparestoreprices.co.uk

www.dooyoo.co.uk

www.priceguideuk.com

www.computerprices.co.uk

www.kelkoo.co.uk

www.pricerunner.co.uk

Property

www.fish4homes.co.uk

www.rightmove.co.uk

www.yourmove.co.uk

Search engines

www.altavista.com
www.ask.co.uk
www.google.co.uk
www.yahoo.co.uk

Software

www.download.com

Travel

www.expedia.co.uk
www.travelocity.co.uk

Well-known online shops

www.amazon.co.uk
www.comet.co.uk
www.dixons.co.uk
www.hmv.co.uk

www.argos.co.uk
www.currys.co.uk
www.harrods.co.uk
www.virgin.co.uk